José Moliner
16 of August 1987.

José Moliner
16 of August 1987.

Spain

Luis Carandell

Spain

Jorge and Jaime Blassi

INCAFO

Text by Luis Carandell
Photographs by Jaime and Jorge Blassi
Copyright © 1980 by Υ INCAFO, S. A. - Castelló, 59 - 28001 Madrid - Spain
All rights reserved

Second edition 1982
Third edition 1986

Publisher: Luis Blas Aritio
Editor-in-Chief: Margarita Méndez de Vigo
Design: Jorge and Jaime Blassi
Translated into English by Sarah Nicholson
Color reproduction by Cromoarte, S. A. - Barcelona
Printed by Julio Soto. Av. de la Constitución, 202
Torrejón de Ardoz - Madrid
ISBN: 84-85389-22-0
Legal deposit: M-25536-1980

Printed in Spain

Contents

COSTA VERDE

RIAS ALTAS

18-19

OVIEDO

28-29　10

LA CORUNA

14-15　34-35　LUGO

31

LEON

27

26　22-23

24

RIAS BAJAS

PONTEVEDRA　ORENSE

30

50

ZAMORA

51

SALAMANCA

60　6

70

PORTUGAL

ATLANTIC OCEAN

CACERES　78-79

BADAJOZ

116-117

SEVILLE

HUELVA　114-115

102-103

105

112-113

COSTA DE LA LUZ

104　91

CADIZ

106-107　120

CEU

The numbers refer to the photographs location in the book

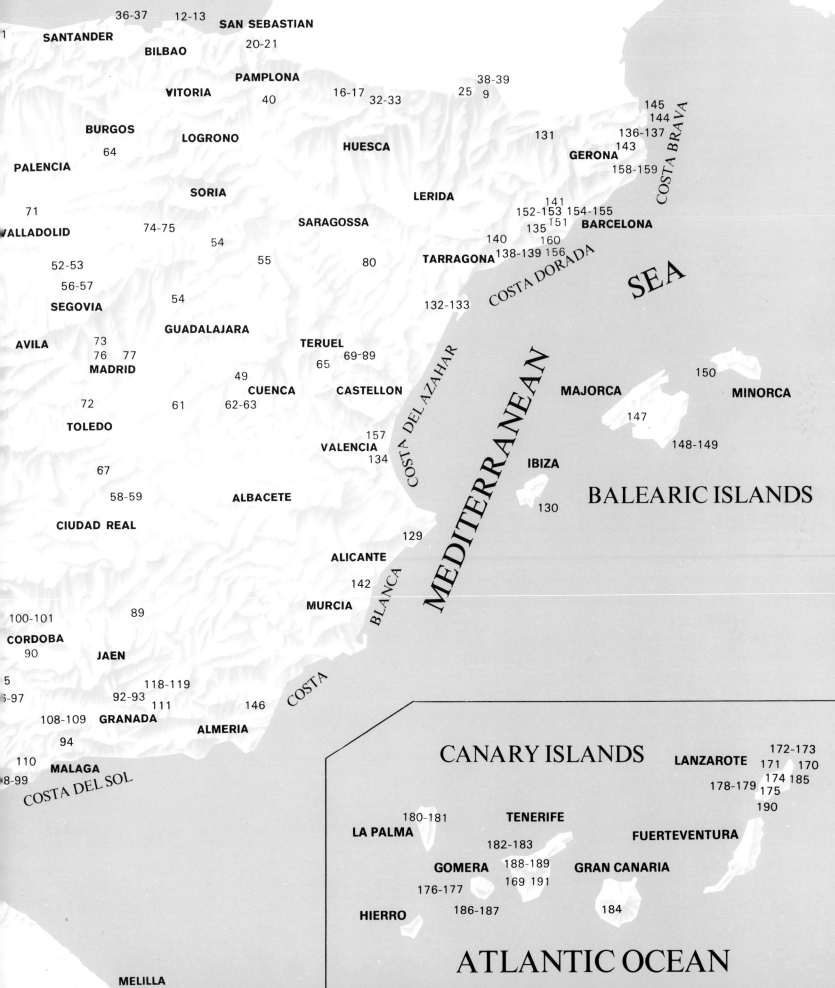

FRANCE

SANTANDER
36-37   12-13   SAN SEBASTIAN
BILBAO
20-21
PAMPLONA
VITORIA
40   16-17   32-33   38-39
25   9
BURGOS   145
LOGRONO   144
64   HUESCA   131   136-137
PALENCIA   GERONA   143
SORIA   158-159
71   LERIDA   141
VALLADOLID   74-75   SARAGOSSA   152-153 154-155   COSTA BRAVA
54   135 151 BARCELONA
52-53   55   80   140   160
56-57   TARRAGONA 138-139 156
54   COSTA DORADA   SEA
SEGOVIA   132-133
GUADALAJARA
AVILA   73   TERUEL   150
76   77   69-89   MAJORCA   MINORCA
MADRID   65   147
49   COSTA DEL AZAHAR   148-149
72   61   CUENCA   CASTELLON
62-63   IBIZA
TOLEDO   MEDITERRANEAN   130   BALEARIC ISLANDS
157
67   VALENCIA
58-59   ALBACETE   134
CIUDAD REAL
129
ALICANTE
COSTA BLANCA
142
100-101   89   MURCIA
CORDOBA
90   JAEN
118-119
5   COSTA
6-97   92-93 111   146
108-109 GRANADA
94   ALMERIA   CANARY ISLANDS   LANZAROTE   172-173
110   171   170
MALAGA   178-179   174 185
8-99 COSTA DEL SOL   175
190
180-181   TENERIFE
LA PALMA   FUERTEVENTURA
182-183
GOMERA   188-189   GRAN CANARIA
169 191
176-177
HIERRO   186-187   184

ATLANTIC OCEAN

MELILLA

Green Carpet

9

A stone wall closes the Land of Spain to the north. The photograph shows the mountain called *Els Encantats,* in the Aigües Tortes National Park, part of the Pyrenees lying in the province of Lérida, and whose name evokes legends of witchcraft.

10

In Asturias, like Scotland, the bagpipe best interprets the depth and mystery of the landscape.

11

In recent years the «descent from Sella», from Arriondas to Ribadesella, has become an international canoeing competition.

12-13

The Basque coastline is dotted with lovely fishing villages, such as Lequeitio, where the motley play of many colors is blended by the light of the Cantabrian sky.

14-15

Galician gastronomy consists of smoked pork and sausage pies, octopus *a feira,* seafood, «nipple» cheese and many other foods. Green Ribeiro wine is always drunk in a cup. The photographs show the menu of a typical picnic outing.

16-17

The town of Fragen, set in the Pyrenees of Huesca, does not seem to have greatly changed for hundreds of years.

18-19

More than any other city, La Coruña conserves its glassed-in galleries which receive the midday sun and are used both as solarium and greenhouse by the buildings' dwellers.

20-21

A beech grove in the splendid forest of Irati, in northern Navarre, scene of ancient legends. Not far from here lies the town of Zugarramurdi where, centuries ago, a famous witch trial was held.

22-23

One of the most authentic — and almost savage — festivals held in Spain is the so-called *rapa das bestas* in which wild horses are sheared. Those who take part in it must put all their strength and dexterity into play. In the photograph, the *rapa* in La Estrada, Pontevedra.

24

Granaries raised on pillars are the most characteristic structures of Galicia. Some of them date back to very remote times and can be considered true works of art. In the photograph, a raised granary in Combarro, Pontevedra.

25

The Church of San Clemente in the town of Tahull in the Pyrenees of Lérida has been referred to as «a stone jewel». The marvellous frescoes in Barcelona's Romanesque Museum were originally from here.

26

The landscape of Galicia's ocean inlets, such as the one in Arosa, is often crowded with devices for catching and breeding mussels, the most popular of all mollusks.

27

Shellfish gatherers on Galicia's ocean inlets provide Spanish markets with savory «fruit of the sea» that add a distinctive note to the menus of fine restaurants, especially those of Madrid which, given its excellent sea food, is considered «Spain's major sea port.»

28-29

During the Upper Middle Ages, Asturias saw the flowering of fine pre-Romanesque art. In the photograph, the magnificent church of Santa María del Naranco, near Oviedo, where weddings are now often celebrated.

30

The Sanctuary of San Esteban de Ribas del Sil, one of Galicia's architectural jewels, rising above a huge rock that overlooks the breathtaking Sil gorge.

31

The romantic setting of the Pazo de Oca, property of the Duke and Duchess of Medinaceli, evokes the world of Ramon del Valle Inclan's *Sonatas.*

32-33

The Ordesa National Park, in the Pyrenees of Huesca, has natural wonders such as the *Faja de Mondarruego* where the Tozal de Mallo summit has a vertical wall that is a challenge to scalers.

34-35

Santiago de Compostela has been a place of pilgrimage since the Middle Ages. The word «pilgrim» was only used to designate those who travelled to visit the tomb of St. James the Apostle, while those who went to Rome were called «Romers», and «palmers» those who voyaged to Jerusalem.

36-37

Santillana del Mar, «the most beautiful town in Spain», according to a character in one of Jean Paul Sartre's works. Near the town lie the caves of Altamira.

38-39

This breathtaking view of the Alto Pallars of the Pyrenees, covered with snow year round and with large growths of Pyrenean pine, can be seen from Lake Naorte. In the background to the left of the photograph looms the peak of Estats, the highest summit in Catalonia.

40

«January 1, February 2, March 3, April 4, May 5, June 6, July 7, San Fermín»: the words of this popular ballad would have us believe that the first six months of the year are merely spent in preparation for Pamplona's important festivals in July.

11

24

36

37

As a beginning to this brief account of the country we call Spain, I would like to propose a voyage to the reader. It is a simple voyage, within the reach of any motorist, and will allow him to appreciate more directly and without the need for long explanations the tremendously varied landscape of the Iberian Peninsula.

Our point of departure will be the town of San Vicente de la Barquera in the province of Santander. The traveller may find it difficult to pull himself away from the many charms of this lovely fishing port: its sleepy streets, the small town square where branches of the trimmed plane trees—as in so many other cities and towns of the North—entwine and form a green roof, the beauty of the town church where a famous Inquisitor is buried, and the quality of the restaurants which serve fish brought in by the boats every afternoon to be sold at the public auction hall.

From there—from the edge of the sea, that is—on a clear day we can see as far away as the Picos de Europa, covered with snow during the greater part of the year, and to all appearances an impassable barrier. As to its climate, this part of Cantabria has worse fame than what the facts actually show. It is true that many days begin rainy and overcast, but it is also true that the clouds that form at night along the mountain ridges slowly scatter as the day goes on, and the sun bursts through the bluish hue of the Cantabrian sky.

Now wending through the town and up the steep road behind—stopping to look at it again from the heights above—, we drive west to Unquera where we turn off the road to Oviedo and begin the seemingly impossible adventure of penetrating the imposing rock wall facing us. A few kilometers further down, the car must make its way along the disquietingly narrow road to La Hermida.

This is one of the most beautiful and most awesome spots in Spain, only comparable to the deep gorge of Trespaderne near the Cares River in Burgos or to the Chorro gorge in the province of Málaga which open up in the steep sierras of the Peninsula, although it is much longer than either of these. For 25 kilometers we pass between the canyon's rock walls, feeling our way around the curves and trusting the road as our Ariadne's thread to lead us through this labyrinth.

Below, at the bed of the Deva River, the enormous rocks that fell from the cliffs and were hedged there by glaciers during the Quaternary Age: local legends tell us that they are «tear drops» of heroes and giants. Small bridges conduct us at least four times over the river (a geological stone cutter that managed to slice open a path in the massif), and narrow tunnels carved in the rock lead us back to the road. At some points the valley widens slightly as if to concede a long-delayed explosion of vegetation. At other places the gorge is so narrow that our world seems reduced to a mere cleft in the rock, with the river at our feet and a blue band of sky above our heads.

At one of these widening points, toward the end of the passage, lies the village of La Hermida which has an inn where excursionists and salmon fishers lodge. Farther along, at the end of the gorge, a small valley tucked between mountains awaits us: its delightful Visigothic hermitage of Santa María de Lebeña has a carved Celtic stone on its altar and at its door, in this amazing microclimate, olive and yew trees grow, both the most southern and most northern of European trees.

From here many possibilities open up to us: at a short distance, we have the village of Potes, ancient capital of Liébana and doorway to the Picos, from where we can visit the sanctuary of Santo Toribio, a place of traditional pilgrimages. Through the town of Espinama where the Marquis of Santillana, one of our great medieval poets, made the flowers of the valley the «accomplices» of his mountain lovemaking, we reach Fuente Dé, with its State-run National Inn, where a cable lift takes passengers up to the refuge of Aliva. From here excursionists can follow the path to see the Lloroza circus ring, Peña Vieja or Torre de Llambrión, with its view of the impressive and almost inaccessible Naranjo de Bulnes peak.

THE ROAD TO SANTIAGO

But our voyage must now take a southern route if we want to find further confirmation of the variety of scenery so characteristic of the Peninsula and which we have already witnessed in little more than an hour's drive that took us from the edge of the sea up to ski stations and mountains rising up three thousand meters. By the San Glorio mountain pass we reach the province of León; by the Piedrasluengas pass, the province of Palencia. And in either case, after a short drive, we find ourselves in the Land of the Fields, the opposite pole of what we have seen on our journey up to now.

Here the only intrusion in the vast open sky are the row upon row of poplar trees stretching out in the distance, forming the perfect image of the «sad and spacious Spain» whose beauty was sung by Fray Luis de León. Earth-colored adobe towns preserve as precious treasures the Romanesque churches that line the Road to Santiago: Frómista, Villalcázar de Sirga, Carrión de los Condes or Sahagún in León, to cite only a few.

In these Gothic fields, as they have been called, we shall end our «pilot voyage» (to borrow a marketing expression) whose purpose was to illustrate the prodigious mosaic of landscapes in Spain. But, for those seeking contrasts, this is not by any means a unique voyage. The Iberian Peninsula is a high pentagonal-shaped promontory that seems to be hanging from the western branches of a Eurasian tree: to cross it from any point on the coast, one must necessarily travel over the high sierras that lead to the Meseta, or central tablelands, and then make one's way again over the mountains that crisscross it from North to South and East to West.

Spain is the most mountainous country in Europe, with the exception of Switzerland, and as such it is not surprising to find such a rich variety of scenery. While throughout history the Pyrenees constituted a natural barrier that isolated the country from the European continent, similarly the Peninsula's mountain chains, from the Picos de Europa to the Sierra Morena and Sierra Nevada, from the Iberian cordillera to the Portuguese Sierra de la Estrella, have separated its different parts creating a «country of countries» in a mosaic not only of landscapes but also of people, culture and even languages for which an advanced system of regional rule had to be designed.

And so our travels could have offered us contrasts as striking as those we have just described if we had driven up from the orange groves of Valencia to the pine forests of Cuenca; from the fields of Catalonia to the deserts of Aragon, whose only source of fertility is the water from the Ebro River which gives its name to the Peninsula; from the Basque meadows to the high tablelands where cereals are grown; from the untamed coasts of Portugal to the ancient oak groves of Extremadura, or from the Andalusian coast, mirador of Africa and melting pot of cultures, across the fertile fields of the Guadalquivir, and from the olive groves of Jaén to the Sierra Morena and the reservoir of water and wine which we call La Mancha.

Inhabited since remote times, the ancient Hesperia of the Greeks or Hispania of the Romans (meaning «land of rabbits» like those we so often see jumping out in front of our car wheels) frequently confuses history with legend. According to one legend, this is the land where Tubal, son of Jafet, settled, meaning that Noah is our grandfather and Spaniards are therefore members of his «virtuous» family.

But this is nothing in our log of time compared to the Catalonian legend whereby God spent the Spring of Creation in the land of Ampurdam or *Empordá,* which owes its name to the Greek and Roman colony of Ampurias. Or the Galician legend which claims that the Creator, tired from his work, sat down on the high Iberian promontory just after he had finished separating the earth from its water and rested his hand on the coast of Galicia, thus forming the estuaries there with the tips of his fingers.

Several kilometers from La Coruña at the end of the small peninsula where the city rises up, stands what is called Hercules' Tower and which (although it seems Roman) is believed to have been built by the strong semi-god during one of his journeys to the Galician coast. In the Christian Era another legend—much more deeply rooted in popular belief than the others—tells us how a stone boat landed at the estuary of Padrón from the Holy Land with the body of St. James (Santiago, in Spanish) the Apostle. We can still see the promontory where the boat landed and from where pious hands carried the Saint's holy remains to what would later be the prodigious temple of Compostela.

ELEPHANT CEMETERY

But we needn't look to legends to lose ourselves in the night of time of this ancient land. In the Guadalquivir valley the remains of human inhabitants dating back a million years have been found. Near Medinaceli in Soria there is a cemetery of elephants with bones and tusks associated with the weapons of their paleolithic hunters. The banks of the Manzanares River near Madrid are one of Europe's richest paleolithic deposits. In the Cantabrian region a rosary of caves with rupestrian paintings are evidence of the extraordinary art of paleolithic times. Aside from the Altamira Caves, which Abbot Breuil referred to as the «Sixtine Chapel of Quaternary Art», there are also the caves of Santimamiñe in Guipúzcoa, those of Castillo or Las Monedas in Santander, or the most recently discovered, the cave of Tito Bustillo in Asturias, baptized with the name of the young speleologist who first explored it.

Beginning in such distant areas and in Spanish neolithic times (which left the eastern half of Spain dotted with towns such as Los Millares in Almería and with friezes painted in the rocky shelters from Alpera in Albacete to Cogul in Lérida) history has accumulated vast evidence of past cultures: the traveller cannot but feel immense delight as he contemplates this rich heritage but, given its abundance, he may also be overwhelmed by it.

There is hardly a town in Spain, or in any event no city large or small, that does not have some testimony of the past worth visiting. This is not a characteristic of Spain alone but of all Old World countries, especially those with Greek and Roman pasts, and of many other countries as well. While in modern times we have unfortunately witnessed the destruction of many sites, both urban and rural, there are still a great number of places in Spain that have remained intact either because they lie in less developed regions where inertia has put a hold on new building plans or because the efficiency of officialdom, whose presence is never overly noticeable, has in spite of all managed to protect them.

It is far from our intention to turn these pages into a dry catalogue of names, even though they may all deserve mention at least once in a list of Spain's artistic treasures. We should warn the reader that when we speak of architectural treasures, we refer not only to monuments (and, as such, they are usually listed in guidebooks) but also give top priority to the popular architecture which constitutes such an important but often neglected part of the patrimony of our cities and towns.

Consequently we shall side-step such major buildings as the Alhambra in Granada, one of the most beautiful structures in the world, and the Mezquita in Córdoba, one of the finest Islamic mosques ever built. We shall skip the great cathedrals of León, Burgos, Toledo, Barcelona, Seville with its svelte Almohade Giralda, or Santiago de Compostela with its glorious Pórtico de la Gloria. We shall forget the Monastery of El Escorial, a perfect work by Juan Herrera, unfairly scorned at times for purely political reasons. Or the Cistercian monastery of Poblet, the finest example of Catalonian Gothic architecture. Or those major works such as the aqueduct of Segovia or the walls of Avila which appear abundantly in books and postcards.

We shall turn our sights to more obscure beauties, less well known to the «public at large,» more modest in one sense but nevertheless appreciated by art lovers. While we shall not, of course, totally neglect the cities and shall try to point out their lesser known aspects, we shall give preference to the towns. One of Spain's basic traits is precisely the beauty of her towns. In other countries large urban centers have sprawled out and absorbed the outlying towns, turning them into mere satellite neighborhoods of the city. In Spain this has not occurred, and while travelling along our country's roads we still encounter delightful towns. There are naturally towns whose native sons, like Cervantes in *Don Quixote,* do not want to remember the name of their place of birth and when we ask them where they're from, will give the name of the capital of the province or the largest town near their own. Other towns, in contrast, are still a source of pride to those born there.

THE «LADY OF THE SOULS»

It has become fashionable to talk about towns, to take to the highways to discover them, to buy old houses in them and to play at looking for «the prettiest town in Spain.» On the Hit Parade of towns, two or three—Santillana del Mar in Santander, La Alberca in Salamanca or Albarracín in Teruel—are always at the top of the listings. We must keep in mind that if Spaniards, so given to enthusiastic superlatives, call one town «the prettiest in Spain,» it does not mean that they will not in the next breath lavish the same title on yet another town.

Of the three towns I have mentioned, Santillana is the most majestic, with the façades of its stone houses bearing coats of arms suggesting highland nobility, with medieval towers and a magnificent collegiate church. As a favorite tourist spot not only for its own merits but also because the Caves of Altamira are only a few kilometers away, Santillana del Mar has several hotels and a National Inn (whose name, by the way—Parador de Gil Blas de Santillana—, is historically incorrect as apparently Lesage's famous Gil Blas was not from this town, but rather from Santillana de Campos in the province of Palencia).

«Smoke keeps houses going,» affirms a popular saying, indicating that uninhabited houses where no smoke rises from the chimneys are the most likely to deteriorate. In contrast to other towns, abandoned by their inhabitants little by little, Santillanans have remained, devoting themselves primarily to agriculture and livestock, and their presence guarantees the preservation of the area. Visitors there are inevitably surprised to find women at the doorways behind tables, neatly covered with tablecloths, selling milk and the rich biscuits that are the specialty of the town.

Albarracín, at the foot of the Montes Universales, in the province of Teruel, will surely make an impression on visitors driving up the road to the town tucked in the hill and surrounded by walls built by a Moorish king. The town square with a small mirador, the narrow streets, the reddish brown of its façades made Albarracín a favorite of Zuloaga (one of the great Spanish painters of modern times, he was enamoured of small towns and lived in the town of Pedraza in the province of Segovia).

La Alberca is the most rural of the three towns we have mentioned. It is located to the south of Salamanca in one of the Peninsula's most beautiful spots, nestled among oak trees and chestnut forests.

La Alberca not only conserves its popular architecture—buildings of wood and clay—but also its traditions, festivals and typical costumes which the older folk still wear. There, every afternoon the *Moza de Animas* («Lady of the Souls») still makes her way through the streets of the town singing her repetitive chant asking for alms and prayers for the souls of the dead.

This is a privileged region. After seeing La Alberca, the traveller will want to drive up to the Peña de Francia («Cliff of France») which can.be reached by a narrow road virtually cut out of the mountainside, with a steep precipice below, to visit the sanctuary of the Virgin. It is said that she appeared to a French lay friar (whose nationality has nothing to do with the name of the Cliff itself, of obscure origin) who was called Simón Vela, a name in Spanish that evokes a somnolent person who had to be reminded by his superiors to stay awake. Following the same road we arrive at a place called Las Batuecas whose monastery has a lovely park where, by the way (and, I believe, this is the only case of its kind in Spain), women are not allowed to enter. «Are you accompanied by ladies?» asks the monk peering through the peephole in the garden door.

Popular architecture is particularly beautiful in the region of Salamanca and the neighboring Extremadura. But, if we were to continue on this road we would reach Las Hurdes, with its harsh legend and reality, where we would feel little aesthetic uplift at the sight of its towns, their one-storey houses covered with slabs of slate, with few new buildings among them, and which seem almost to be one and the same with the landscape.

A PORTUGUESE CITY

The province of Cáceres, like Salamanca—my typewriter growls at me for having neglected to mention the marvelous town of Candelario, near Béjar—is especially fortunate with respect to the conservation of its popular architecture. We can see it in towns in the Jerte Valley or the valley near Plasencia with the charming name of Garganta la Olla (roughly «Kettle Throat») where, according to ancient romance ballads, the *Serrana de la Vera,* the famous man-eating highland woman, lived. The architecture is particularly outstanding in

Gothic Fields

49

Autumn colors of the black poplars alongside the Júcar River wending its way through the city of Cuenca.

50

The procession of the Calvary of Bercianos de Aliste in Zamora is one of the most austere Holy Week celebrations. Penitents cover themselves in the white cloth that will one day be their own shrouds.

51

The façade of the Catedral Nueva de Salamanca, a perfect example of plateresque style, a true «stone lacework.»

52-53

The Castle of Coca, one of the most complete structures of military architecture. On the route of Segovia's castles, aside from Coca, other castles which should be seen are those of Cuéllar, Turégano, Castilnovo, Pedraza and the Alcázar of Segovia.

54

The grey land of Soria and red earth of Guadalajara. The tablelands of central Spain provide splashing contrasts of color.

55

The Horse's Tail is the name given to the huge cascade at the Park of the Monasterio de Piedra, a fertile region that looms up almost like a miracle in the arid land of Aragon.

56-57

Perhaps the best engineering work left by the Romans on the Iberian Peninsula, the aqueduct of Segovia brought water to the city until recent times. It has been called «the stone harp.»

58-59

The wheat fields of the tablelands of central Spain might be compared to the sea, and thus we even hear them referred to as «the sea of wheat.» Blown by the wind, the vast wheat fields sway back and forth imitating the rising and falling of ocean waves.

60

La Alberca, in Salamanca, conserves its lovely popular architecture and ancestral traditions, such as the custom of the «Moza de Animas», a woman who walks through the streets of the town every afternoon singing psalms for the deceased.

61

In Almonacid del Marquesado, Cuenca, a festival called *La Endiablada* («Devil's Masquerade») is held every February. The men of the town dress up as devils and bishops and jangle huge cowbells in honor of San Blas.

62-63

Looking up from the gorges of the Júcar and Huécar rivers that surround Cuenca, we contemplate the castle-like city in which all the houses seem to be hanging on the edge of a precipice.

64

Of all of Spain's great cathedrals, perhaps the most graceful and most spiritual is the Cathedral of Burgos.

65

The Towers of Teruel, such as the Tower of San Martín, are marvellous jewels of Mudejar architecture combining checkered brickwork with the green and white ceramics of its crafts tradition.

66

Fighting bulls grazing in the meadows surrounded by evergreen oaks in the province of Salamanca offer one of the most beautiful and characteristic scenes of the ancient peninsula.

67

The traditional celebration of Corpus Christi is kept alive in the city and province of Toledo. The town of Camuñas continues to put on a religious play in which all the roles, including that of the «Madama», are enacted by men.

68-69

The painter Zuloaga was the «discoverer» of the town of Albarracín, a prodigy of popular architecture rising above a hill surrounded by walls constructed by a Moorish king.

70

Hog slaughtering is an inevitable peasant ritual. In La Alberca, Salamanca, the traditional method of cleaning swine by burning them with ferns is still practiced.

71

Behind lovely façade of San Gregorio, in Valladolid, lies the magnificent National Museum of Sculpture which contains the country's best collection of Spanish religious carvings.

72

Holy Week is Spain's major festival, and it is widely celebrated.

73

Set in the austere landscape of the Sierra del Guadarrama, the Monastery of El Escorial — «eighth marvel of the world» to Spaniards — evokes the figure of King Philip II and his great architect, Juan de Herrera.

74-75

The Castilian countryside undergoes prodigious changes in the different seasons of the year. Cinderella in winter, parched and dry in summer, reddish in autumn, in spring she dows a tunic of flowers.

76

The Buen Retiro park, in the center of Madrid, conserves the serene classic elegance of the days of the House of Austria. In the photo, the Crystal Palace and the pond with the statue of Alphonse XII overlooking it are shown.

77

Madrid's prodigious growth in recent years brought with it ultra modern architectural setting which, if at first seemed out of place in the old part of town, have now acquired a personality of their own.

78-79

The great Renaissance architecture of the town of Trujillo, in the province of Cáceres, blends with the popular style of the buildings on the outskirts. The statue of Francisco Pizarro, the most famous of its native sons, looks over the proud setting.

80

The major characteristic of Holy Week in Aragon is the so-called *Tamborrada.* The whole town participates in the deafening uproar of drums which on the nights of Holy Thursday and Friday symbolize the cataclism that shook the earth when Christ died.

49

54

64

65

73

74

76

78

the towns of the region called La Vera, located on the southern slope of the Sierra de Gredos. In Cuacos, in Villanueva or in Valverde de la Vera, the streets, with grooves formed by running water, are as narrow as secret passageways and are almost covered above by the closeness of the balconies and eaves. Villanueva celebrates fiestas such as *Pero Palo,* an old tradition whereby a doll baptized with this name is paraded around the town receiving the invectives of the inhabitants. Valverde, as we shall mention later in reference to Holy Week, still celebrates the ancient tradition of *Los Empalaos,* where one encounters the strangest and most mortified of penitents. In La Vera handcrafts are made that have yet to be discovered by crafts lovers. Shepherds still make beating mortars using the very hard wood from the roots of the ash tree.

The visitor to La Vera should also plan side trips to Jarandilla, with its Renaissance palace converted into a National Inn, and to Yuste, the somber monastery where Emperor Charles withdrew to die, and whose rooms have been reproduced with more or less respect to historical truth. This does not, by any means, end the list of interesting towns in the province of Cáceres but, if all their names were given, this book might easily become an unwieldy manual. There is still room, however, to mention the monumental town of Trujillo where Pizarro was born; Plasencia, built by Alphonse VIII with the instructions—and thus the name of the town—that «it be pleasing.» And Guadalupe, a town nestled around a monastery, and where coopers still carry on their craft.

It goes without saying that by choosing Cáceres as representative of Extremadura, we did not intend to neglect Badajoz where the breathtaking Roman city of Mérida may so fascinate the visitor that he leaves no time for seeing other places. Other towns—although rather than towns we should speak here of small cities because in Spain the further south we go, the farming towns become increasingly larger—deserve a longer visit. This is the case of Zafra, which has the finest castle in all of Extremadura. Or Jerez de los Caballeros with its splendid towers. Perhaps the traveller would appreciate the recommendation that he not leave Extremadura without visiting a small Portuguese city in Spanish territory: Olivenza, which Portuguese nationalists still lay claim to, arguing that it was usurped in past wars. The houses decorated with tiles, just as some of its popular traditions and especially the music of the *corridiños,* all testify to Olivenza's origin. And until a short time ago Portuguese was spoken there.

GONZALO DE BERCEO

If I had to choose a town that best represents the popular architecture of Old Castile, the first to come to mind might be Frías, set on a hill in the shape of a boat and with a turreted castle as a finishing touch. Frías has an almost tragic look, as if it had been left to dangle loosely in the air. The region to the north of Burgos where Frías is located has marvelous landscapes. The Ebro River flows down from Reinosa following a questionable origin in Fontibre (actually its first source of water is the peak called Tres Mares—«Three Seas»—which owes its name to the fact that a drop of water falling there may just as easily have come from the Atlantic, the Cantabrian or the Mediterranean), and then opens its path over a stone wall. Towns in the middle of practically nowhere, such as Pesquera de Ebro, at the bottom of an almost inaccessible valley, surprise us with their manorial houses with coats of arms. Another, Orbaneja del Castillo, is barely more than a fine line of houses perched between two rock walls. Farther up, the river crosses the cheerful valley of Valdivielso, almost meridional in its vegetation.

Beyond Miranda, the Iberians' ancestral river enters the land that a classic poet, Esteban Manuel de Villegas, called «red and happy Rioja,» Castilian only through an official division, for it is very different from the land surrounding it. From Haro, a wine capital, to Calahorra (a fertile area which nonetheless was famous in ancient times for the famine it suffered during a devastating siege of the city), the Rioja region has earned fame in Spanish agriculture not only for producing Spain's best wines but also for the quality of its vegetables, from bitter peppers to delicious asparragus.

In Rioja we cannot bypass Santo Domingo de la Calzada, and not only to visit its cathedral where there is a chicken roost hewn in stone where live birds nest. This roost was built in memory of a miracle performed by Saint Domingo who resuscitated a young boy and, at the same time, brought back to life the stewed poultry he had eaten for lunch, thus giving rise to the saying: «Santo Domingo de la Calzada, and the hen that crowed after being stewed.» From here we take a turn-off to the road leading to the monastery of San Millán de la Cogolla, in the foothills of the Sierra de San Lorenzo.

Very near San Millán lies Berceo, the town where Gonzalo de Berceo, the first poet to write in Castilian Spanish, was born. The *portaleyo* where he wrote his long poems—in verses «like rows of poplars,» as Machado noted—can still be seen at the monastery of San Millán de Suso, or de Arriba. The caretaker of

Suso, Tarsicio Lejárraga, an admirable Riojan and greatly fond of the monastery, gladly recites Berceo's verses to visitors.

In San Millán de Yuso, or de Abajo, an anonymous monk of the 10th century wrote the *Códice Emilianense* which contains the first phrases written in Castilian Spanish that have been conserved. It is also interesting to note that the same codex contains on another page the first phrases written in the Basque language. Again crossing the sierra, we may want to stop at the Monastery of Valvanera where one can also find lodging. And from Anguiano, a town famous for its festival in which young men donning colorful tunics walk down a steep hill on high stilts, we come to Salas de los Infantes where a small chest that is never opened conserves the heads of the Seven Infantes of Lara.

In our search not so much for great monuments as for small surprises, we might now visit the Visigothic hermitage of Quintanilla de las Viñas, the delightful town of Covarrubias and, if possible, the amazing ruins of the Monastery of San Pedro de Arlanza. From here we shall go to the religious community of Silos to contemplate once again the centuries-old cypress of its cloister and hear, if we coincide with vespers, the monks' Gregorian chants. Beyond Silos there is a spot well worth visiting: a natural cleft in the mountain rock, parallel to the tunnel on the main road, called Yecla. To visit it we must leave the car at the entrance of the tunnel and descend on foot down an extremely narrow opening where a wooden passageway has been built. Water seeps from the walls and trickles down to the river below. Above, we can make out the zigzag line of the sky. To return to the car we must go back over the road through the tunnel.

Very close by is Caleruega, birth place of another Saint Domingo, this time Santo Domingo de Guzmán, founder of the Order of Preachers, with its lovely palace converted into a convent. From here it does not take long to reach Peñaranda de Duero, one of Spain's best conserved monumental towns. In its square, closed off by the church and the Avellaneda palace, there is a lovely round Gothic column—or «log»—of hewn stone. These «logs» were territorial milestones and were also used as pillories. The condemned were tied to them on large iron rings, some of which can still be seen, and exposed to public shame.

THE ANCIENT PHARMACY

Right off the square lies the ancient Ximeno pharmacy which still belongs to the same Ximeno family that founded it three hundred years ago. It has a lovely collection of ceramic jars from Talavera with inscriptions such as Gentian, Belladonna, Hemlock, Crab Eyes and Deer Priapus (the latter to cure impotence). In the back room the pharmacy still conserves the small laboratory with its original grinding mortars, still, spatula board and scales. Beyond it there is a small garden where medicinal herbs were cultivated.

There is still ground to cover in this region, and very close by lies the town of Coruña del Conde. On the outskirts we find the ruins of a Roman city, Clunia, from which the town derives its name. But the glories of Coruña del Conde are not its classic background alone. A shepherd by the name of Diego Martín was from this town and several years ago the Ministry of Aviation dedicated a small monument to him that can be seen from the road. The shepherd, apparently a very inventive man, conceived the idea of flying and, with the help of the town blacksmith, built a hulk with articulations over which he mounted wings covered with feathers. If we are to believe the ancient account of the story, on the night of May 11, 1798, after years of hard work, Diego Martín put his project into practice. With the help of his brother and the blacksmith, he hauled the airplane up to the castle and taking his seat in the apparatus, announced: «I'm going to Burgo de Osma and from there to Soria. I'll be back in a few days.» An ancient manuscript tells that he reached an altitude of five *varas* (around 14 feet) and that he was seen flying in the moonlight, but that after advancing some five hundred Castilian *varas,* he fell on the other side of the river. It is said that Diego Martín, who became the blank of his neighbors' ridicule, died of sadness at the age of forty-five.

What in Castile is stone and adobe, in Aragon is brick and it still spins in the hands of the grandchildren of the Mudejar architects who built the towers there. What distinguishes Spain from other countries of the continent is the coexistence of great European art—Romanesque, Gothic and Renaissance—alongside Mudejar art of Arab origin. The Mudejar style can be found in many regions of Spain, but in the towns and cities of Aragon it found its greatest intimacy with the landscape. The color of the buildings of Calatayud, of the graceful tower of Ateca, to cite only two of the extremely abundant examples of this art, blends so harmoniously with the color of the desert landscape of Aragon that it is hard to tell where the land ends and the work of man begins.

If I had to choose an example of Aragonese Mudejar, perhaps I would point to–after mentioning Saragossa's Aljafería and Cathedral or the wonderful urban setting of the town of Tarazona–the towers of Teruel with their daring play of brick and green and white tiles that glitter in the afternoon sun. Also lovely are the towers of the Cathedral and the Church of San Pedro where the famous Lovers of Teruel are buried («silly she and dumb he» goes the popular expression, thus putting a damper on this romantic legend). But Teruel's two best towers are those of San Martín and El Salvador which, according to tradition, were built simultaneously by two Arab architects who were competing for the love of a beautiful Moorish woman.

THE DEER THAT PLUNGED OVER THE CLIFF

But we are in Aragon and it would be unforgivable to bypass the province of Huesca and thus miss one of the loveliest sites in Spain. We shall start in Jaca, a military city from long ago which conserves intact its citadel from the epoch of Philip II. From here we can reach the Monastery of San Juan de la Peña by way of a paved road that wends around the southern part of Monte Pano. It would be wiser, however, to take the road from Jaca to Pamplona and then, a few kilometers from there, turn off at the sign indicating Santa Cruz de la Serós. The Church of San Caprasio, with its octagonal tower, is a very original example of Romanesque art. But the truly unusual and unique surprise lies ahead on the top of the mountain, which we ascend by a dirt road for some seven or eight kilometers.

Arriving at San Juan de la Peña, the traveller will feel no less awed than the legendary hunter named Voto. As the legend goes, he chased a deer to the top of the Pano mountain, and when the animal reached the edge of the rock with a steep drop, it wasn't able to stop and so fell into the void. Voto descended the mountainside and found a deep cave in a shady setting with oak and ash trees from where the snowy slopes of the Pyrenees on the other side of the valley could be seen. Voto interpreted the deer's death as a sign from heaven, for had the deer not plunged over the precipice, the cave would never have been discovered. He expressed his thoughts to his friend Félix and together, way back in the 9th century of the dark Middle Ages, they decided to build a monastery in the very place where the deer had fallen.

There are hardly words to describe the marvel of San Juan de la Peña: added to the original primitive construction, which can still be seen, are structures of all imaginable styles which history's different stages converted into a pantheon of the Monarchs of Aragon, a dwelling for monks and the tomb of well known figures of modern Spain such as the Count of Aranda, the 18th century reformist. Neither the most precise description nor the best photograph could give even a hint of its beauty. We shall have to content ourselves with pointing out that the monastery's roof is the rock of the deep cave discovered by Voto, forming an earth-embedded shelter over the cloister with its seemingly divinely inspired architecture.

Looking now for a contrast of opposites, we make our way to La Mancha, none of whose towns—to judge by the inscriptions we read upon entering them—is resigned to be excluded from the prestigious Route of Don Quixote. Some of them, however, conserve a particularly Cervantesque atmosphere. Wandering through their streets, it takes little effort to imagine the Ingenious Hidalgo, dressed in armor, appearing at one of these doors, painted blue or sienna, along the line of houses with their long white walls, as he ventured out to set aright the wrongs of the «perverse and monstruous» world.

In La Mancha the towns are white and the eaves of the roofs are rounded by uncountable coats of lime applied throughout many centuries. The quintessence of La Mancha can be found in towns such as Campo de Criptana with its wind mills, Argamasilla de Alba, with its famous jail where Cervantes was held prisoner, and especially El Toboso where the village woman Aldonza Lorenzo lived and whose beauty Don Quixote was willing to defend with his life.

We are in a region famous for its wines, where the towns' subsoil is completely perforated with wine vaults and cellars built centuries ago. Tomelloso, Daimiel or Valdepeñas, all wine-growing capitals, are good examples of this. Just as there is an abundant tunnel of wine running beneath the towns of La Mancha, the entire region also forms a subterranean water cistern. The Guadiana River that crosses it might be said to have the most personality of any of the Peninsula's rivers. It starts in the lagoons of Ruidera, a series of lagoons appearing at intervals which receive their name from the strange «noises» (*ruidos,* in Spanish) which Cervantes attributed in his literary fiction to the enchantments of Merlin the Magician. In its course and still near its source, it submerges beneath a mill known as La Membrilleja, and later reappears at a considerable distance away in a place called Ojos del Guadiana, near Daimiel.

TABLAS DE DAIMIEL

The name of the Guadiana River is used literarily in Spain as a symbol of those things, or even people, that disappear from the political or cultural scene or any other area of social life only to reappear at another point in time. The same water which crosses La Mancha and gushes out at Ojos del Guadiana somewhat further down its course forms one of the Peninsula's most important humid zones, a stopping place for migratory birds on their annual trek from northern to southern Europe: the Tablas de Daimiel, near the town of the same name. The word *tabla* means a sheet of water and conveys the sensation of the quietude of Daimiel's moors: the stillness of the water filled with marshland plants, such as ditch reed and rushes, is only broken by the sudden rise to flight of red-crested pochards, mallards or coots flapping their wings as they skim the water.

As an ecosystem the Tablas de Daimiel are less important than other areas of the Peninsula, especially the Ebro Delta and the great natural reserve of the Coto de Doñana on the marshlands of the Guadalquivir River, one of the largest in Europe. But the Tablas de Daimiel—spreading over a surface of some 1,800 hectares—are one of the most attractive and original landscapes in central Spain and make a marvelous excursion. The warden of the Tablas, Bautista García Consuegra, is a man entirely dedicated to the conservation and defense of the Daimiel ecosystem. He will also accompany visitors, and may even invite them to join him on a ride on one of the flatboats (modeled after those used in the Ebro Delta) so appropriate for travelling on shallow waters such as the Tablas. A journey across these waterways and shoals, where the nearby hills are reflected as if in a mirror, heightens our awareness of Nature in its pure state and provides an aesthetic pleasure second to none.

The Isla del Pan, the Isla de los Asnos and other tiny territories where tamarind-like trees grow and where small herds of sheep graze near the ruins of a pavillion once used for royal hunts, all give us the deep impression that time has stopped. Bautista's flatboat leads us through the reed mace of the marshes to spots whose names he knows as well as we know those of our streets and squares. Here bird watchers can spot some of the thirty-eight species of birds that nest in the Tablas as they rise in flight over the water. During part of the year coots, mallards and red-crested pochards from Lapland share this habitat with birds whose name alone indicates their beauty: avocets, spoonbills, teals, grebes, lapwings, black-winged stilts, marsh harriers, black-headed gulls...

The Kingdom of Lime

89

Jaén's olive groves owe their geometric beauty to the fact that they are a man-made landscape. More than tillers of the soil, the peasants here have been the involuntary architects of their own scenery.

90

Pottery making still plays an important role in Spain. There are few regions that do not offer examples of this ancient craft of working in clay. In the photograph, a potter in the town of La Rambla, Córdoba.

91

There are few towns in Spain like Setenil de las Bodegas in the Cádiz mountain range. The houses, built on rocks, stand in line beneath the cornice of the olive grove.

92-93

Nothing matches the Alhambra, one of the four or five most beautiful buildings in the world. An Arab poet wrote: «Here I forget Baghdad and Damascus. I have never seen such a beautiful place any where».

94

In her landscape and architecture, in her festivals and customs, Spain is also a stepping stone between Europe and Africa.

95

Holy Week in Osuna, Seville. Here the celebrations are baroque and grandiose.

96-97

The splendor of the Sevillian countryside against the blue of the sierra. On the side of the mountain, the town of Estepa.

98-99

Rising out of the hill, Casares is one of the most beautiful towns in the sierra of Málaga. Its houses are a perfect example of centuries-old traditional popular architecture and, nonetheless, they seem avant-garde. What wouldn't modern architects give to have invented something like this!

100-101

The Mezquita of Córdoba, one of the finest examples of Islamic architecture, stands as a witness to the splendor of the Caliphate.

102-103

The El Rocio *romería* (traditional excursion) in the marshland of the Guadalquivir draws hundreds of tousands of participants each year. The center of the festivity is the Virgin who is popularly known as «The White Dove».

104

Carthusian horses are nearly one the same with Andalusia, Jerez de la Frontera and the Fair. This horse, from the Terry stud farm, has a name well suited to its bearing: *Descarado II* («Brazen II»).

105

Little by little the dunes of the Coto Doñana invade the pine grove. The contrast of light and color reach their maximum expression here. This is one of the regions in Spain where nature has been most preserved in its purest state.

106-107

Several towns on the coast of Cádiz, and Barbate in particular, still practice the method of fishing tuna with nets. Boats surround the school of tuna fish which has just crossed the Straits. There is no escape for any of them.

108-109

Archidona, in Málaga, is the quintessence of an Andalusian town. In the center, the famous Plaza Ochavada.

110

Ronda's bullring has deep roots in Spanish bullfighting tradition. Called the «conservatory of Tauromachy,» it was here that Pedro Romero set down the modern-day rules of the bullfight. In the background, the mountain range of Ronda, famous for Pinsapo fir trees, a species of pine dating back to the Quaternary Age.

111

With the breathtaking backdrop of the Sierra Nevada, the town of Güejar Sierra preserves intact purity of its Moorish origin.

112-113

The Coto Doñana is an immense nature reserve, as suggested by the flock of thousands of flamingoes flying over the marshlands there. The Coto is a vital stopping place for birds on their annual migrations between Europe and Africa.

114-115

In the Andalusian countryside, scenes of pursuit and felling are both cause for a celebration as well as a completely necessary stage in breeding fighting bulls.

116-117

Along with Holy Week, another major festivity in Seville is the April Fair. It began as a livestock fair and has since become a synonym of the gaity and hospitality of Andalusia.

118-119

Caves are still used as dwellings in the provinces of Almería and Granada. The town of Guadix in Granada boasts the largest of these «troglodyte» neighborhoods. Cave dwellers are extremely proud of their living quarters.

120

From the mountain pass of Cabrito, the craggy coastline of Morocco beyond the Straits of Gibraltar can be seen. Spain's closeness to Africa is always a source of amazement.

90

106

110

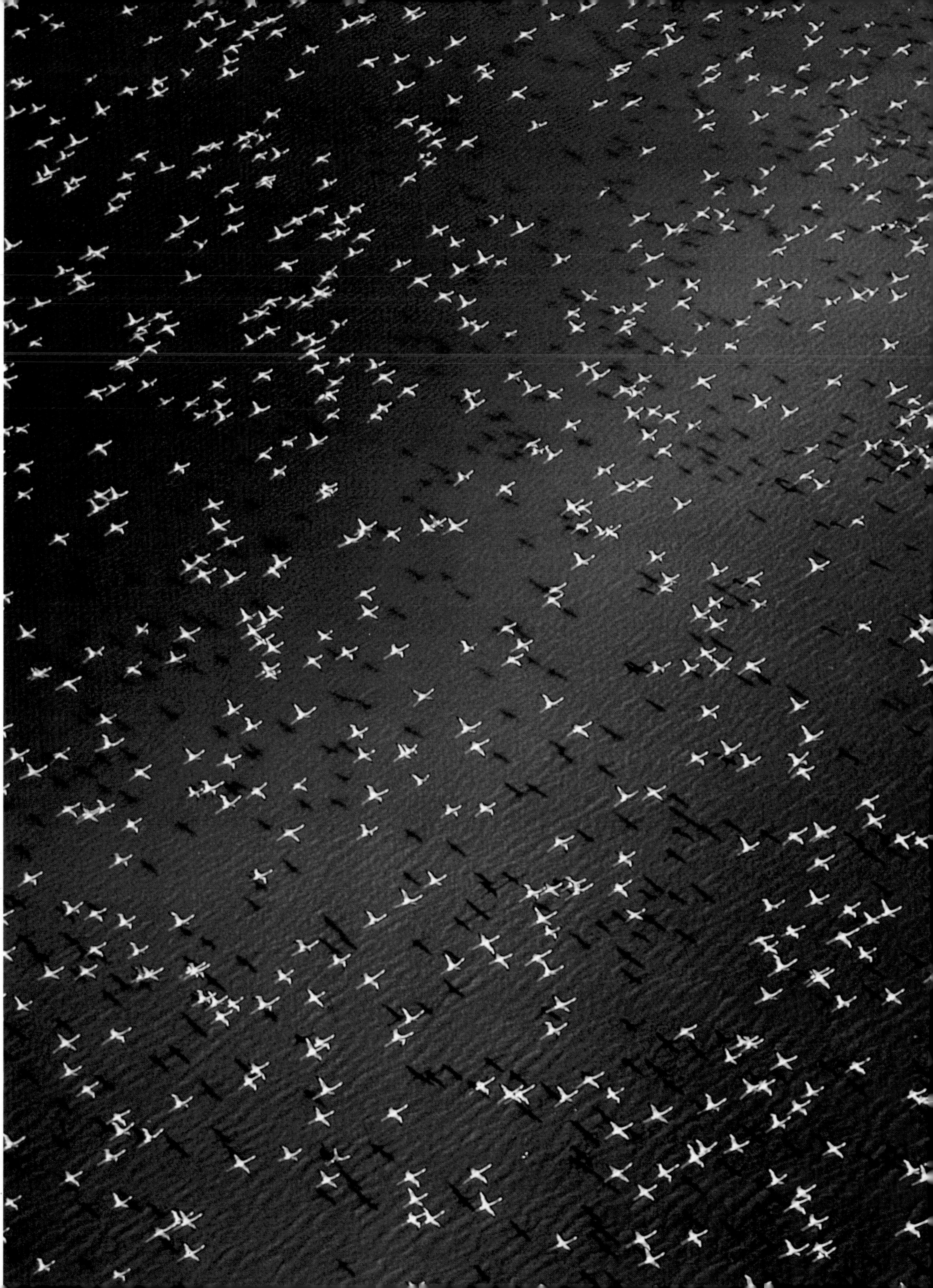

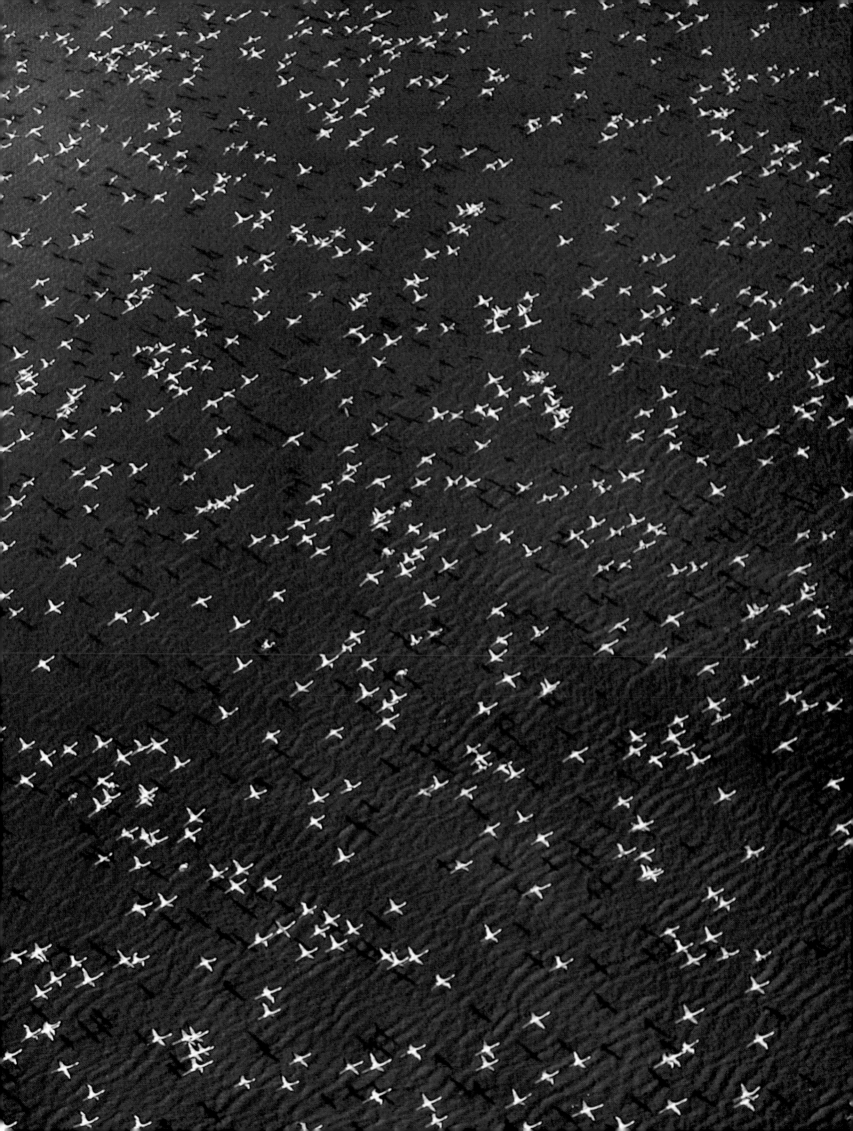

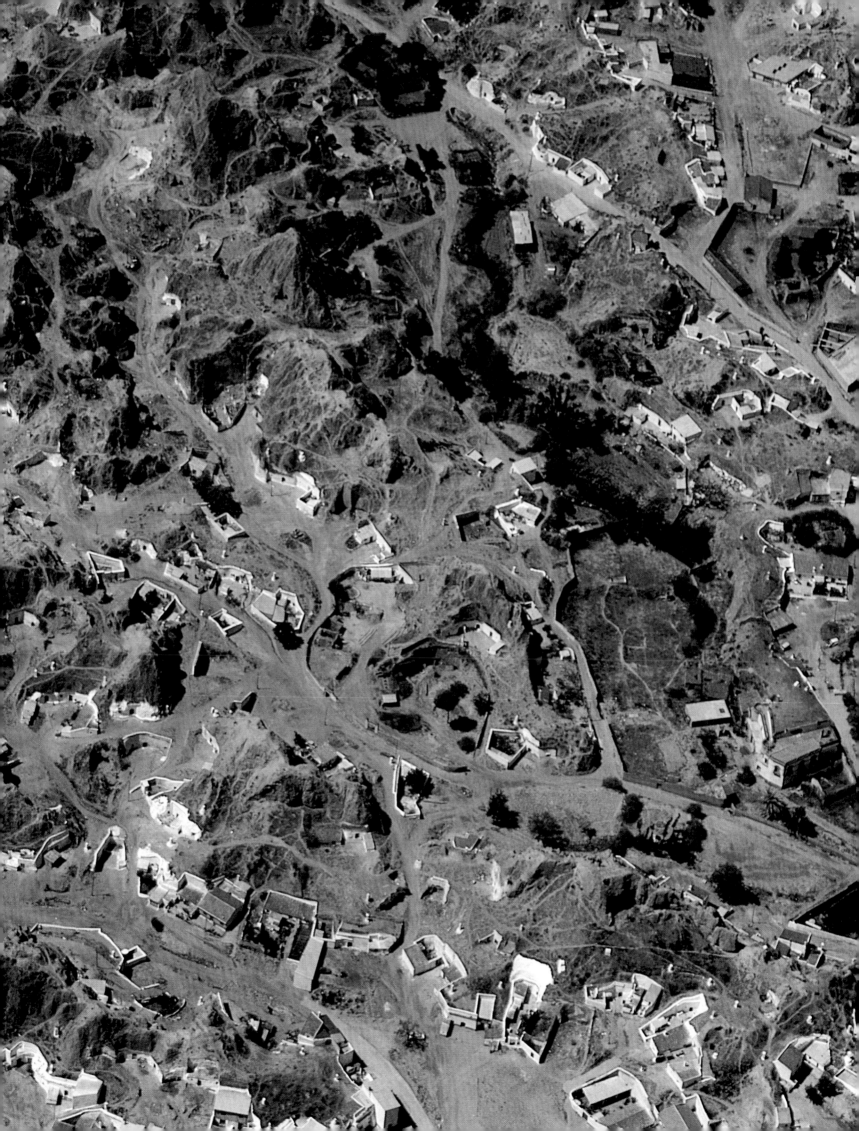

120

Not far from Daimiel, before leaving La Mancha, we shall visit the town of Almagro, with its extremely elegant main square formed by rows of houses with glass-enclosed porches and beams painted green. In one of them there is a 17th-century theater, perhaps the most ancient in Europe, in a perfect state of conservation and where works by Calderón and Lope de Vega are still performed.

As in all the towns of La Mancha, in Almagro the white of the lime-washed façades is predominant. But this is merely the prologue of what we shall see in Andalusia, whose whitewashed walls extend resplendently from the Portuguese border to the beaches of Almería. In Spain the custom of whitewashing is strictly a women's affair. We often see them in La Mancha and Andalusia sternly dressed in black, splashing lime on the façades. Towns in the province of Cádiz such as Arcos, Vejer or Castellar de la Frontera are called «the white towns.» Little need be added to give an idea of their whiteness, if we remember that here we are in the kingdom of lime and only an exceptional white earns the adjective «white.»

SOUTH OF GRANADA

In the Aracena Sierra, dominated by the deep green of holm oak groves, the towns scattered about the mountain slope strike us with their stark and immaculate whiteness. A string of memories comes to mind recalling the feast to the traveller's eyes when, from what is called the Peña de Arias Montano (where the famous humanist of this name retired during the reign of Philip II), he contemplates the town of Alájar at his feet. Or the almost ghostly vision, bathed in the light of the Atlantic, of the town of Moguer where Juan Ramón's silvery Platero frolicked. And the amazing luminosity of Cádiz, the towns of the Sierra de Sevilla, Córdoba's hermitages tucked among orange and lemon trees, Ecija's towers with their shining cupolas, Jaén's fields where Machado looked out «among the olive trees and white farmhouses.» Or the Alpujarras, described long ago by Pedro Antonio de Alarcón, and whose best contemporary interpreter is the English writer Gerald Brenan, autor of *South of Granada,* who lived in towns of this region for twenty years.

In the Sierra Nevada, with the Peninsula's highest mountains and crossed by a road that has the highest altitude of any in Europe, there are lovely valleys such as the Poqueira gorge with its towns of Pampaneira, Bubión and Capileira that we can contemplate from above, with their cubic architecture of flat roofs covered with impermeable soil called *launa.* Or the valley where the town of

Trevélez lies between orchards flanked by mountains nearly three thousand meters high. Trevélez, unmistakably Moorish in its architecture, is famous for its ham which is cured in the Sierra.

What is most amazing about the Sierra Nevada is that next to these towns with their marked rural character that still conserve traces of their original Berber inhabitants, the region offers the chance to go on wonderful excursions to the peaks of Mulhacen or Veleta or to go skiing at resorts with ultra modern installations and, on the same day, to have a swim in the mild waters off the coast of Granada and Almería.

In eastern Andalusia, between the provinces of Granada and Almería, there is a succession of towns that might be most aptly described as «cavernous» were it not for the scornful-sounding edge of this adjective. Located on the mountainsides, these towns—and especially the neighborhoods rising up in the higher parts—have countless caves that are still inhabited. Although there is no doubt that the region's poverty is an historical factor that led people to recur to such primitive lodgings, many still remain there out of tradition and attachment to their whitewashed and spic-and-span dwellings, neatly decorated with flowers. Guadix, an episcopal city with lovely Renaissance buildings, has perhaps the Peninsula's most well known «troglodyte» neighborhoods, but it is not by far the only one. Some of these towns, such as Cuevas de Almanzora («Caves of Almanzora»), take their name from the singular dwellings found in this region of Andalusia.

As we travel through Almería we often get the feeling that we have left the continent of Europe altogether and are taking in our first glimpse of Africa. Here there are deserts where certain areas can point with pride, if not to rich «harvests,» at least to a flourishing movie industry where «Spaghetti Westerns» are produced. The sea is turquoise blue and the towns are Moorish, including such places as Carboneras, San José and, above all, Mojácar, one of the best preserved towns on the entire Spanish Mediterranean coast. The contrast of the scenery as we rise toward the north is once again striking: running parallel to sandy deserts there are extremely fertile orchards alongside the Segura River. I am now reminded of the beauty of Murcia's fields that can be seen from the hill where the Sanctuary of the Virgen de la Fuensanta, near Murcia capital, lies, or the landscape that can be seen from the miradors overlooking the orchard fields of Orihuela in Alicante.

It would be impossible to even mention in passing the port towns of interest along the Mediterranean coast, probably the most well known region in Spain.

From Cabo de Gata to the north, the building at tourist sites has greatly modified the original setting and, at the same time, has given these towns and cities a new life. At Cabo de Palos lies the Mar Menor, an interesting natural phenomenon where a tongue-shaped stretch of land, now very urbanized, forms a peaceful ocean inlet with tranquil beaches and several peculiar species of fish such as the striped mullet used in Murcia's exquisite fish dishes.

A SHORT TRIP TO FLAMENCO SONG

Not far away lie the mines of La Unión and the city of Cartagena, Hannibal's Carthago Nova. By mentioning La Unión we recuperate an important aspect of our popular culture: flamenco song with all its infinite variations. In La Unión *tarantos,* or miners' songs, are sung, whose restrained emotion and often painfully sad words make them sound like plaintive moans from beneath the earth. The *cartagenera* is a lighter song, while the *jabera* is heart-rending and extremely difficult to sing. Going back over the same road—i.e., from east to west—we find the *malagueña* (of which the *cartagenera* and the *jabera* are offspring) as well as the songs of Granada, the so-called *granaina* and *media granaina.* The *malagueña* has lovely variations such as the *verdiales* and the *malagueña del Mellizo.*

Flamenco is not exactly folk music if by this we understand music composed and sung by anonymous native sons. It is definitely song «with a signature.» The name of the *cantaor,* or singer, who invented each song or gave a new turn to an older form is always remembered. *Cante grande*—the *seguiriya* and the *soleá,* for example—consists of gypsy songs that are also sung by *payos,* or non-gypsies. According to a theory as radical as it is firmly rooted, *cante grande* corresponds exclusively to the geographic triangle formed by the cities of Seville (and more concretely its Triana neighborhood), Utrera and Jerez de la Frontera. *Cantaores* from this magic triangle don't give the time of day to outsiders: «Those people have never sung,» they'll tell the traveller, referring to «foreigners» from other towns.

Cádiz has lighter but extremely lovely songs such as *bulerías, alegrías* or *tanguillos.* Huelva has the enormous variety of the fandango, with the specialities of Huelva, Valverde, Alonso, Almonaster and Santa Eulalia. Among the specifically gypsy songs is the *alboreá,* a wedding song that non-gypsies not only never sing but, by ancestral tradition, are not even authorized to listen to.

The so-called *petenera* is one of the most beautiful of all songs, especially the *petenera grande,* attributed to the great flamenco *cantaora* named La Niña de los Peines. It is a Hebrew song («Where are you going, lovely Jewess, so composed and at this untimely hour? I am looking for Rebeco who is in a Synagogue.») with a solemn melody and words that often express religious or philosophical thoughts.

EUROPE'S DATE PALM GROVE

We shall return to the towns of the País Valenciano when we speak of Spain's festivals, for they are particularly lively in this area of the Peninsula. We shall mention Alicante's lovely mountain town, Polop de la Marina, tucked in the Sierra de Aitana, and which is not far from the touristy Benidorm or from the white Altea. Here again we find a sharp contrast between flourishing industrial and agricultural cities such as Elche, called «Europe's date palm grove,» and the arid land of the interior, just as the rich farming towns of Valencia contrast with the mountain wilderness that separates it from the Meseta. From the orange groves of Castellón we rise to the hills of Teruel and travel across the territory known as El Maestrazgo whose capital, Morella, abounds in memories of the Carlist wars. Or, in an especially brusque change of landscape, from the Ebro Delta to the desertlike lands of Aragon through which the Ebro River opens avenues in the rocks, or to the mountains of the Catalonian Priorato, where the Peninsula's thickest wine is produced.

In spite of its dense population and high level of industrialization, Catalonia has lovely towns. I am reminded of Montblanch, a walled fortress not far from the Monastery of Poblet in Tarragona province; the city of Seo de Urgel in Lérida province at the doorway of Andorra; Vallfogona in Barcelona where a famous priest, taking after Quevedo, wrote his piquant and scatological verses; Vich, the farming city that is worth a visit on market days and whose cathedral, decorated by Sert, has immense frescoes in gold and sepia; or, in the province of Gerona, the medieval town of Besalú or the towns in the region where the Greek and Roman city of Ampurias is located and which gives its name to the marvelous territory known as Ampurdam.

The Costa Brava, in spite of its many tourist buildings, has conserved much of its charm. Tossa de Mar, Calella de Palafrugell, Llafranc or Bagur still remain partly as they were. But, beyond any doubt, Cadaqués is the coast's best preserved town. It owes its protection not only to the fact that it is isolated—in the almost lunar region near Cabo de Creus—but also to the fact that certain members of Catalonia's enlightened bourgeoisie have taken special pains to conserve it.

If I had to choose a town representative of Catalonia's inland area, intact from remote times, I would undoubtedly think of the village of Tahull in the Pyrenees of Lérida. Located on a promontory, until very recently it could only be reached by a dirt path that is now a road. This town of stone and slate has two churches—Santa María and San Clemente—that are the best examples of the Pyrenean Romanesque style. Their small size, almost hermitages, with the finishing touch of graceful human-scale spires, makes me want to describe them as works of a goldsmith more than architecture. Both churches are jewels in the most concrete sense of the word, and the second one—San Climent, as it is called in the Catalonian language—has truly prodigious frescoes with the large figure of the Pantocrator presiding over them. The original frescoes were moved to Barcelona's Museo Románico years ago but, much to the visitor's delight, they were first faithfully reproduced on the church walls.

«LOS JAMEOS DEL AGUA»

The names of many towns, of places all worthy of recommendation, clammer at my typewriter struggling for at least a word of mention in this impressionistic vision of Spain.

I can almost hear reproaches from the names of towns that have yet to find their way to the typing keys, among them some of my favorites, such as Osuna in Seville; Ronda in Málaga; Ubeda and Baeza in Jaén, or Sigüenza in Guadalajara, Burgo de Osma in Soria, or—not far from the Pyrenees of Lérida where we now are—Sos del Rey Católico where Ferdinand of Aragon was born, with its fortress enclosure filled with palaces that are reached through the doors of the ramparts.

Now a peninsular interlude will allow us to make the jump to the islands to select representative spots and dispel the idea that we have forgotten them. In the Balearic Islands we shall not mention the all-too-well-known stalactites and stalagmites, or the Carthusian monastery of Valldemosa, where as everyone knows Fédéric Chopin and George Sand sought their lovers' refuge, though few remember that the brilliant poet Rubén Darío, staggering in drunken creativity, also spent time here. We shall skip over the cosmopolitan Ibiza and the primitive Formentera, with its delightful architecture, and we shall set our sights on the Island of Menorca, impregnated with English tradition, with its Golden Farm where Nelson lived. Not far from its lovely beaches, still solitary even on certain days in summer—which is saying quite a lot—there are megalithic monuments over three thousand years old, known as *Taulas*, huge stones placed on top of one another in table-shaped arrangements that were apparently meant to represent the bull in ancestral cults.

In the Canary Islands we shall leave the Orotava valley and the unique view of Teide which, according to Humboldt, is the «most beautiful landscape in the world,» and the beaches where, in winter and summer, retired Europeans go to rest, in order to visit Lanzarote, an arid volcanic island where camels must often substitute the car on our excursions. There, in the midst of its inhuman landscape we find sites as surprising as the so-called Cueva de los Verdes, a long canal formed by the gases of the Corona volcano, or what are called Jameos del Agua, an underground lagoon where an odd species of white crab lives which has no eyes for its life has always been spent beneath the earth.

If we could travel on the Peninsula as easily as we move a pointer from one spot to another on a map, we would now travel to the Cantabrian cornice beginning in the Pyrenees of Navarre with its high valleys of Baztán and Roncal, where we find marvelous forests, such as Irati, and towns such as Zugarramurdi which bring to mind the Witches' Sabbath. Or mountain passes such as Roncesvalles where Moors from Saragossa—or, according to a more nationalistic version, the Basque *gudaris*—defeated Charlemagne's valiant knight Roldan, whom French chauvinists have never allowed to die with one deathblow but rather relate that his veins burst when he attempted to sound the horn of war to warn the armies of his lord.

The Basque coast, the most densely populated area in Spain and also heavily industrialized, nonetheless still conserves pleasant small cities such as Fuenterrabía and fishing towns such as Guipúzcoa's Guetaria where Juan Sebastián Elcano was born (he was the first navigator to travel around the world), or the Biscay towns of Ondárroa and Bermeo in whose surroundings we find a hermitage called San Juan de Gaztelugatxe that can only be reached by a passageway carved out of the rock that emerges from the sea and which is accessible only on calm days.

The abundance of water in the Cantabrian area doesn't mean its inhabitants abstain from wine. In Basque towns and cities there is a firmly rooted wine-drinking custom called *chiquiteo* or *poteo,* generally the exclusive domain of men who go from tavern to tavern to order *chiquiteos* or *poteos,* words indicating the size of the wine glass and which Basques have converted into verbs—*chiquitear* and *potear.* Santander's fishing towns are similar to those in Guipúzcoa or Vizcaya, with their harbors filled with vibrantly colorful boats, greyish houses with red roofs, squares with bandstands where music is played and stone collegiate churches with marine symbols on their spires. Castro Urdiales and Laredo are like this, with their ancient *puebla,* or old sections, in spite of new constructions, as well as Colindres and Santoña, and, beyond the city of Santander, San Vicente de la Barquera of which we have already spoken.

«Asturias, beloved country, Asturias of my loves, who could be in Asturias, at certain times»: this is the typical song invariably sung by busloads of excursionists. It is a sort of «national hymn» in a lower key. Some Asturians even take seriously what is usually said jokingly: «only Asturias is Spain and all the rest is conquered land.» The more or less legendary and even apocryphal Don Pelayo, who defended the Goths' fortresses in the cliffs of Covadonga from the conquering Moslems, is the principal person responsible for our national existence. We must thank his descendants for such Romanesque marvels as Santa María del Naranco, which was used as a palace by King Ramiro, Santa Cristina de Lena or the so-called «Conventín» of Valdediós, where King Alphonse retired when he was dethroned by his sons.

LAND OF LEGENDS

On the Asturian coast there are lovely fishing towns such as Cudillero, located on a tiny inland bay where boats form traffic jams at the entrance. But we are now in Galicia, the region least influenced by the Romans in Spain, which still conserves the secret aureole of its Celtic legends of witches, specters and *Santas Compañas* that appear at night to solitary travellers. Valle Inclán wrote about the region's turbulent existence, just as Rosalía described its most delicate sentiments so well. Galicia has lovely cities such as the monumental Orense and, of course, Compostela; delightful towns such as Betanzos, the jewel of Mariñas, with the three jewels of its churches of Santiago, San Francisco and Santa María do Azougue (in front of the latter there is a lovely *cruceiro* of the many that abound in Galicia).

On its coastline there are deep bays that are like inland seas where the fishing is good and which is also the source of virtually all the shellfish that is eaten in

Golden Mare Nostrum

129

The façades of Alicante's Villajoyosa display spontaneously decorative colors whose greatest charm lies in their unplanned distribution.

130

Few images of Spain are so well known internationally as the sight of the city of Ibiza. For all her cosmopolitan airs, the capital of the Pitiusas archipelago has lost none of her primitive charm.

131

Every year on Corpus Christi Day, the town of Berga in the province of Barcelona holds what is called *La Patum*. The giant figures represent Christian and Moorish kings.

132-133

This photograph was taken in La Cava, a town in the Ebro Delta. The owner of the house makes fishing gear and is a barber and picture framer as well.

134

The *Fallas* of Valencia is perhaps Spain's most famous festival, if not the most «resonant» as well, for the uproar of fireworks is a constant element of the fesitivities. Craftsmen work all year long constructing the sculptured figures that, in one night, will be burnt to ashes. Only a chosen few are granted pardon from the flames.

135

The tradition of *castellers,* or human castles, finds its origin in the town of Valls, in Tarragona. Here the *xiquets* build their tower in front of the Town Hall of Vilafranca del Penedés.

136-137

Throughout history the Monastery of Sant Pere de Rodes, near the Greek and Roman settlement of Ampurias, has been the spiritual center of Ampurdan.

138-139

Giant headdresses — called *capgrossos* in Catalonia — together with giant figures are an inseparable element of Catalonian festivities. The oddest characters imaginable are likely to appear.

140

In the Tarragona contryside a *llaurador* can still be seen using centuries-old methods to plow the plot of land alongside his farm house.

141

From the town of Monistrol the awesome cliffs of Montserrat can be viewed. This «mountain-shrine» is Catalonia's sanctuary.

142

At the *Huerto del Cura* («Priest's Orchard») in Elche, referred to as «Europe's date palm grove», the most succulent specimens of this fruit can be found.

143

Alongside the banks of the Oñar River, the old section of the city of Gerona preserves its primitive charm.

144

Cadaqués is one of the best preserved towns on the Mediterranean coast. It owes this to its isolated location on an almost inaccessible peninsula as well as to the constant watchfulness of artists, intellectuals and members of the enlightened bourgeoisie.

145

The rocky landscape of Cabo de Creus is a faithful terrestrial image of the moon's surface. In a kind of eiry grandeur, it displays a wide gamut of the mineral beauty of the earth.

146

Spain also has its deserts. And the one in Almería, of which a bird's-eye view appears in the photograph, has been widely put to use by the film industry. This area has been both Texas and Nevada in many a «Spaghetti Western».

147

Palma de Mallorca — *Ciutat* to islanders — is at once a fishing port with all its charm and a striking city. The old part, around its handsome cathedral, is replete with ancient palaces in a setting of evocative streets.

148-149

In the cove of Santanyi, as in many other along Mallorca's coast, the transparency of the water gives us the sensation of unreality or the amazement of seeing that a blue such as this truly exists.

150

The men of Menorca are the protagonists of the splendid festivities of San Juan in the town of Ciudadela.

151

Every year at Christmastime, the Cathedral of Barcelona — Miguel de Unamuno's favorite — witnesses the sale of crèche figurines at the Santa Lucía market.

152-153

At «El Molino», heir of Barcelona's best music halls, the audience takes delight at the piquant naïveté of the cabaret world of the *belle époque.*

154-155

«Happy is the city», wrote Maragall, «that has a mountain nearby for it can contemplate itself from above». Barcelona, seen from Tibidabo, responds to the praise it received from Cervantes when he said that it was «unique in location and beauty».

156

Sitges, in the province of Barcelona, covers its streets with carpets of flowers on Corpus Christi Day.

157

The façade of the palace of the Marqués de Dos Aguas displays the splendor and overwhelming imagination of Valencia's baroque style.

158-159

Calella de Palafrugell, on the Costa Brava, still keeps alive the rich musical tradition of the *habanera* which was introduced in Spain many years ago by Spaniards who had returned from Latin America.

160

The *Drac,* or «dragon», is the center of attention at the festivities in Vilafranca, capital of the wine-growing region of Penedés.

130

143

144

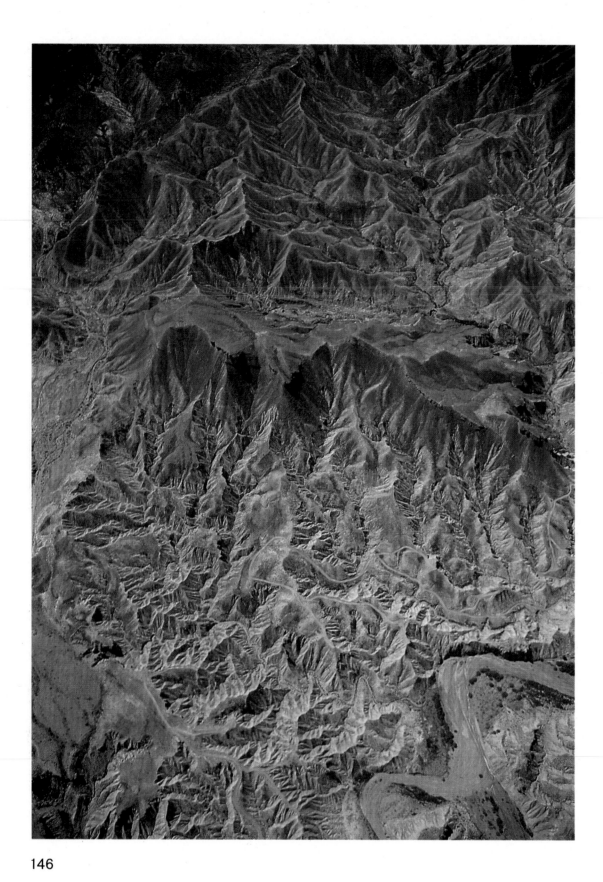

146

Madrid. Such are the advantages of centralism that, from a gastronomic point of view, the capital is still referred to as «Spain's best sea port.» The Rías Bajas are extremely beautiful, graced with towns such as La Guardia or Bayona, spas such as La Toja–now a gambling casino–and beaches such as La Lanzada. But if I had to choose one area of Galicia, it would be the little known and solitary Costa de la Muerte («Coast of Death») which spreads out from the fishing port of Malpica to the westernmost point of the Peninsula. This craggy coast, which seems to jut out too soon from the earth where it opens its flanks from north to south onto the Atlantic, has caused so many shipwrecks that it has acquired its own Black Legend.

It is said that, in the past, inhabitants of the Costa de la Muerte tricked seamen with false lighthouses by setting on fire the horns of cows which they led from one place to another until the boats had run aground. The land that borders the Costa de la Muerte is known as the Comarca de Bergantiños, and it has fishing towns such as Corme, Laxe or Camariñas, where the women still make exquisite lace for which the region is known. Near Muxía, another spot in this land of legends, is the rock that popular tradition identifies as the ship in which the Virgin arrived to visit the Apostle. In Finisterre, near the lighthouse on the western point of Europe, we shall end our journey.

LOWERING THE VIRGIN

The centenary tradition which we have seen conserved in different types of architecture can often be found as well in customs, especially those related to popular festivals, in spite of the migratory movements that have left many places uninhabited and the population of others greatly diminished. At fiesta time, however, emigrants working in Spain's industrial cities or even abroad make special efforts to return to their towns and take part in their festivities. Consequently, such fiestas not only have been conserved but, in recent years, have been given a new impulse.

The festivities of the patron saints of towns and cities are mostly celebrated in summer. No place, no matter how small, unless it is totally deserted, does without its fiestas, which are frequently attended by some important official person or group or special guests drawn by the festival's fame. Among the many celebrations where people let out emotions held back during the rest of the year, there are always processions to move the image of Christ or the Virgin or the Patron Saint from one place to another, usually from the town church to a nearby hermitage where it remains during the summer. Some of these processions, such as the so-called «Lowering of the Virgin» in Valverde (the capital of the Island of Hierro) are spectacular events. Equally so are the seamen's processions held in many coastal towns where gaily decked out fishing boats carry the Virgen del Carmen around the harbor.

Among the fiestas of patron saints—and here we must consciously leave out many others—we shall mention those of the Virgen Blanca of Vitoria which begins when the entire town goes out to watch the typical *celedón* as it is lowered from the tower of San Miguel, and those of the Magdalena in Castellón with its major *romería*, or festive outing. And, speaking of *romerías*, we cannot omit the famous one at Rocío, the great festival of the marshlands of Almonte in Huelva where hundreds of thousands of people arrive in carriages, cars and buses from all over western Andalusia. But there are still other *romerías* in the region. Every spring, the Virgen de los Remedios in Fregenal de la Sierra (Badajoz province) receives a multitudinous gypsy outing very similar to the one celebrated in Saintes Maries de la Mer in the French Comargue.

Sometimes processions take the form of sacred dramas or street dances with townspeople following the religious images. The *Endiablada,* in Almonacid del Marquesado in the province of Cuenca, consists of a group of devils that follow the image of San Blas and which, on the second day of the festivity, change their demoniacal horns for bishops' miters. In Zamarramala, a small town very close to Segovia, two mayoresses are elected to preside over the procession of Santa Agueda. In La Puebla in Mallorca it is San Antonio Abad who is honored. *La Patum,* celebrated in the Barcelona town of Berga, is partly the enactment of a drama, while the Mystery Plays of Obanos (Navarre) and the famous *Misteri* of Elche are pure theater, in which every August an ancient text is enacted inside the church from whose cupola the Angel of the Assumption descends.

Many of these fiestas harken back to medieval traditions. Others are ancestral, such as that of San Pedro de Lequeitio in Vizcaya in which several men carry a platform on which a strange personage known as Katxarranka dances. Corpus Christi has quite singular processions, some of them modern, such as that of Sitges where the streets are covered in a carpet of flower petals, and other older ones such as the multitudinous and luxurious procession celebrated in Toledo when the cathedral monstrance, made by the Arfe brothers, is taken out into the street. In the province of Toledo the town of Camuñas represents an original religious play in which all the characters, including the «Madama», are enacted by men.

CROSSING THE FIRE

Aside from the well known April Fairs in Andalusia and the Carnivals which are celebrated with the greatest to-do in Santa Cruz de Tenerife, Cádiz and Ciudad Rodrigo (not to mention the extremely odd carnival of Lanz in northern Navarre), Spain's major fiestas have three essential components. They are either fire fiestas, or festivities related to bulls or horses. The first are held mainly in the eastern half of Spain, although there are important exceptions to this. The *Fallas* of Valencia are the most famous, but the *Nit del foc* on the night of Saint John is not only celebrated in Alicante but along the entire coast as well. The Fiestas of Moors and Christians are celebrated with the greatest pomp in cities of Alicante and Valencia such as Alcoy, Villajoyosa, Villena, Bocairente and others, although we also find them further south as far as Alpujarras. In Villajoyosa, contending bands not only fight in the town streets but also hold a naval battle and stage an ostentatious landing. Naturally the Christians always win, but among the townspeople who take part in the fiestas the role of Moor is a thousand times more coveted.

The most famous fiesta of this series, held outside the País Valenciano, is the so-called *Paso del Fuego* («Crossing the Fire») held in San Pedro Manrique, in the province of Soria. A bonfire of oak wood is made and when the flames have died out, a sort of carpet of live coals is spread out and men from the town walk over them in bare feet. Frequently they carry a girl, a special guest or the civil governor (if the top provincial authority happens to be to their liking) on their backs. After crossing the coals, they show their feet intact to witnesses. The following day the fiesta of *Las Móndidas* (believed to be the personifications of Celtiberian priestesses) is held.

In Castile, Extremadura or Andalusia, it would be inconceivable to hold a fiesta without bulls. Until a few years ago, some towns in Zamora held a fiesta called «the lanced bull» which consisted of setting a bull loose in a field while young men with lances waited for it. The «Jubilo bull» in Medinaceli had to suffer the torment of pellets of burning tar placed on its horns. All this has now disappeared and what remains are fiestas such as that of the «roped bull» in Benavente, where the animal is roped on both sides by groups of young men and led through the streets. The *encierros* or bull runs—the most famous is Pamplona's San Fermín—with their immense fanfare have special variations such as those of Estella, where not only young men but also young women take part in the run, and those of Soria with ancestral rites. The most ancient bull runs in Spain are held in the town of Cuéllar, in the province of Segovia.

Wild horse festivals are held only in Galicia. In the town of Sabucedo and others, *Curros* are held which consist of the risky task of cutting wild horses' manes, an operation known as *rapa das bestas*. At the opposite extreme—and not only geographically—are the horses of Ciudadela in Menorca, where one of the loveliest festivals of Spain is held. Riders, decked out in black suits and their horses gaily adorned, «take» the city on the day of Saint John, and while the crowds look on, they show off their riding skills and take part in races to pierce rings with long poles. In Balsareny, in the province of Barcelona, the muleteers' fiesta is somewhat similar to the Menorcan festivities just described. We must also include in this chapter the riderless horse races in Caravaca de la Cruz in Murcia. Finally, in Atienza, in the province of Guadalajara in New Castile, a spectacular fiesta called *La Caballada* is held to commemorate an historical episode related to the childhood of Alphonse VIII, the victor at the battle of Navas de Tolosa. When the young boy was at the castle of Atienza, the city was sieged by his uncle King Ferdinand of León who wanted to take over Castile. The muleteers of Atienza carried the child out through the door which is still called *La Salida* («Way Out»), thus tricking the troops from León, and from there took him to Avila on a journey that lasted seven days. When he came of age, Alphonse conceded special privileges to the brotherhood of muleteers which they still conserve. On Pentecost Sunday the members of the brotherhood don wide hats and capes and parade on horseback to commemorate the event.

THE DANCE OF DEATH

Holy Week in Spain offers an interminable catalogue of celebrations that range from the sacred representations such as those of Olesa de Montserrat, Esparraguera and Sant Vincenç dels Horts in Barcelona to the fête of Valmaseda in Vizcaya. One of the most interesting theatrical works of the Holy Week repertoire is the procession in the town of Verges in Gerona that includes a figure called the «Dance of Death» draped in black mesh on which skeletal bones are painted.

In Andalusia, as in Castile, large scenes sculpted by the great baroque masters of religious images are removed from the churches and carried in processions. In the south, processions are more colorful and almost like gay community fiestas. In Castile they are more solemn and moderate, with the exception of Cuenca's famous *Turbas*. In many places there are articulated images that embrace when they meet, or bless the fields. In Pollensa in Mallorca the *Davallament* or Descent from the Cross is enacted.

Holy Week in Aragon is dominated by the strident sound of drums. In Híjar, in Alcañiz or in Calanda the drumming lasts two full days and nights. Townspeople, trained from childhood, don't compete with one another to rise above the din but rather each competes with himself and his own bleeding hands. From the deafening roll of the drums in memory of the moment when Christ died and «the earth opened and the sepulchers opened», we turn to the self-communion and penitence which is practiced during Holy Week in many towns of Spain. The *picaos* that thrash their naked backs in the town of San Vicente de la Sonsierra in the region of La Rioja are an example of the gallery of medieval masochism which also finds expression in a town which we have already mentioned, Valverde de la Vera in Cáceres. There the *empalaos*, crowned with thorns, walk barefooted and carry wooden poles bound to their crossed arms by strong esparto ropes. Bercianos de Aliste (Zamora) holds a procession in which the members of the local confraternity, dressed in the white tunics that will later be their own death shrouds, climb up the path of Calvary. Women and men from the town follow them wearing the typical greyish capes of Aliste. An almoner repeats the chant: «A donation for the burial of Christ, God will recompense you».

A striking contrast are the processions of Lorca and other towns in Murcia which are a true explosion of color, with circus-like images of Tiberius, Anthony and Cleopatra on a carriage, the Assyrian slaves of King Cheops, Nebuchadnezzar and his priests, Cambises, Nero, Alexander and Attila. In Puente Genil in Córdoba biblical figures representing different characters from sacred history parade through the streets. We can easily affirm without any fear of exaggerating that Holy Week is Spain's greatest celebration, her greatest fiesta.

I would not want the reader to draw the impression from what I have written that Spain is a country that lives a primitive life, as might be concluded from what I have said up to now. Precisely what is so characteristic of Spain is the marked difference between urban and rural life, two worlds that coexist separately from each other. This is why I would now like to indicate very briefly several cities that have conserved some of their original life style and personality.

BLIND IN GRANADA

The reader will allow me, for example, to remind him to walk through the narrow streets of Toledo beyond the usual tourist circuits; to go around the city of Lugo above its fortressed walls; to climb to the upper part of Cáceres to see the marvelous architecture of its palaces; to walk around the Espolón of Burgos with the Arco de Santa María facing it, or to walk down the ravines of the Júcar or Huécar contemplating the hanging city of Cuenca above.

Or to go to Madrid's *Rastro* (flea market) on Sunday where what is left of the city's most typical manners and customs can be found; to take a look at the Cava Baja where there are still ancient inns with «travellers and stable clients»; or to enter the old taverns decorated with tiles and the old cafés with marble-topped tables.

To go up the tower of the Cathedral of Oviedo to see the city that Clarín called «Vetusta.» Or to walk through the market at Fontán which is the literary city that Pérez de Ayala called «Pilares.» Or to go to its rival city of Gijón to drink, in Cimadevilla, «panther milk» or draught of alcohol and milk served in wooden jugs.

To walk down Sierpes street in Seville or perhaps enter the small baroque Church of San José; to buy votive offerings in front of the Church of Salvador; to go on the day that gives its name to Seville's Thursday *(Jueves)* flea market; to eat fish in the neighborhood of El Palo in Málaga; to lose himself among the tiny squares of Córdoba; to follow the path of Antonio Machado's daily route «between San Polo and San Saturio» on the banks of the Duero River in Soria.

Or to walk down the Ramblas of Barcelona crowded with people that are perhaps the ultimate expression of modern-day life that can be found in Spain; to visit Pamplona's ramparts; to go through the tiny streets of the Jewish quarter in Palma de Mallorca and, finally, to climb up the path to the Alhambra in Granada, the most perfect of all our historical monuments. In its patio lined with myrtle patches, there is a stone tablet with the inscription of a popular couplet which the traveller might interpret as a true reflection not only of

Granada but of this entire ancient Peninsula. The couplet suggests a scene in which a blind beggar goes up to a man and his wife who are walking through the streets of Granada. The husband—and here I draw to an end—says to his wife:

> Give him alms, woman,
> For in the world there is nothing
> So sorrowful as being
> Blind in Granada.

LUIS CARANDELL

Daughters of Atlantis

169

During the festive outing in Los Frailejos, on the island of Tenerife, guitars give a non-stop performance of *folía,* music typical of the Canary Islands.

170

The scene of a camel yoked to a plow expresses more than any other exotic atmosphere of the Canary Islands, and especially of Lanzarote where this photograph was taken.

171

Lanzarote has been called «the fertile moon» for only through the labor of men has this desolate countryside (Lanzarote's so-called «badlands») been transformed into a region of fertile crops.

172-173

From Mirador del Río in Lanzarote, the coastline with the stylized silhouette of the Isla Graciosa, with its spacious beaches, can be seen.

174

Ancient tales of Lanzarote tell of a Genoan sailor called Lancelot who gave his name to the island. Could he also have been the founder of Teguise, the former capital of Lanzarote?

175

A street in Teguise, the former capital of Lanzarote.

176-177

Valley of the Gran Rey, on the island of Gomera. The tilled terraces on the steep hillsides look like an Asian landscape.

178-179

The salt marshes of Janubio in Lanzarote reflect the bluish hues of the Atlantic Ocean.

180-181

San Miguel de la Palma, enveloped in soft white clouds, watches over nature's wonder, the Caldera de Taburiente National Park.

182-183

The town of Garachico on Tenerife lies on a scant slice of land wedged between the mountain and the sea. At the end of the 18th century, a volcanic eruption blocked off the port and destroyed many houses.

184

During the festive excursions of the towns of Gran Canaria island melodies played on primitive instruments can be heard, and the women's colorful native costumes, worn without folkloric affectation, are a delight to the eyes.

185

On Lanzarote wheat grows on the hillocks men have managed to till on the lava landscape. There is no other way of making the earth fertile.

186-187

The island of Gomera has splendid groves of laurel which is common to the group of islands that comprise Macaronesia, i. e., the Canaries, Azores and Madeira.

188-189

The summit of Teide, on the island of Tenerife. Observing it, the naturalist Alexander von Humboldt exclaimed, «This is the most beautiful landscape in the world».

190

Time does not seem to have lapsed in Lanzarote's countryside where scenes from biblical days still come into view.

191

Red marigolds grow on the volcanic slopes, at times reaching heights of up to two meters. They are also called «glen marigolds» and «pride of Tenerife».

192

The photographic composition on the last page of the book gives us, all in one glimpse, an idea of the infinite variety of the landscape, customs and life style of the country we call Spain.

174

171

170

190

Fiestas of Touristic Interest

WINTER

Fiestas of San Antonio Abad.

La Puebla, Island of Mallorca. Origin prior to 1365. Huge bonfires called *rogueros* are lit in the middle of the streets, while *cançoners del Camp* go through the town singing to the music of tambourines and zambombas; the masked *colla de demonis* dances and sings to the sound of bandurrias, guitars and tambourines, and groups of young men and women, dressed in traditional costumes, perform centuries-old songs and dances. During the fiestas, cattle are led in front of the altar of San Antonio to be blessed.

The Drums of San Sebastián.

San Sebastián, Guipúzcoa province. To the deafening din of beating drums, participants parade through the city on the first night of the fiesta, on the following morning–children drummers–and then again that night to celebrate the Saint's Day of the city's Patron San Sebastián.

Fiestas of Moors and Christians.

Bocairente, Valencia province. Dating from the 16th century. Nine lavishly decked out formations–four bands of Moors and five Christian bands–participate. Large, colorful parades. Harquebus shooting, battles and discussions to dispute the fortress whose castle rises up in the Caudillo square. The procession in honor of the town's Patron Saint, San Blas, is received with cheers at this square, illuminated by the light of candles carried by the faithful. A firework castle is then set off. Each day's festivities are brought to an end by the *Cordá,* in which several couples go through the streets setting off chains of firecrackers until they meet in the Caudillo square which then becomes a brazier of embers.

The «Endiablada.»

Almonacid del Marquesado, Cuenca province. Dating back to time immemorial. Young men of the town dressed up as devils–pants and jackets with loud flowery designs, huge cowbells dangling from belts at their waists, multicolored paper hats, later replaced by cardboard bishops' miters–go through the streets, dance in the church atrium and later inside it, pretend to wash the image of San Blas, and then head the procession in honor of this saint, jangling their cowbells nonstop.

Fiestas of Santa Agueda.

Zamarramala, Segovia province. Very ancient origin. Two mayoresses–who, in effect, supervise the religious aspects of the fiesta–wearing sumptuous 12th-century costumes and carrying the staff of authority, preside over the procession in honor of Santa Agueda. Afterwards, they and the married women of the town, dressed as peasants, hold a meal in which no men except the priest participate. The festivities end with the performance of an ancient circle dance.

Fiesta of the Muleteers.

Balsareny, Barcelona province. Of very remote origin, it consists of the blessing of riding animals, a huge cavalcade of horses decked out in ancient trappings, performances by folkloric groups, mealtime feasts of «typical» muleteer dishes, and horse, mule and donkey races on the uphill race course ending at the town castle; sardanas (a dance typical of Catalonia) and other popular entertainment.

Carnival Fiestas.

Santa Cruz de Tenerife. Street musicians, serenaders and masked merrymakers dance and parade in the streets; lavish cavalcade of carriages, cars with streamers and hundreds of mascaraders filing down the main street; dances at recreation halls; bullfights and contests for the best disguises.

Traditional Fiestas.

Ciudad Rodrigo, Salamanca province. Dating from the 11th century. The major attraction are the typical bullfights, including amateurs behind the capes, especially the bull runs led by mounted riders: bulls are let loose in the streets and frenzily dodged and chased by the young men of the town.

International Barcelona-Sitges Classic Car Rally.

Sitges, Barcelona province. Cars manufactured prior to 1920 take part in this fiesta, driving a previously established itinerary. Participants don clothes typical of the period. Automobile clubs from Spain, as well as from France and Andorra, take part.

«Els Comparses».

Villanueva y Geltrú, Barcelona province. Couples dressed up in costumes, men sporting jaunty caps and women wearing embroidered silk shawls, parade about accompanied by bands of musicians. A spectacular «battle of sweets and candy» is held, as well as the election of a comparsera of honor and child comparsera. Popular parade of masks and disguises.

Spring Fiestas.

Tolosa, Guipúzcoa province. Dating from the 17th century. Festivities start on the Thursday before Shrove Tuesday, although they officially begin on «Drumbeating Saturday.» Then practicing for the «Reveille» gets under way, with the music of the *txistu* (a Basque instrument) playing pieces whose origin goes back to very remote times. The fiesta ends with the celebration of the *Toro del Aguardiente* («Brandy Bull»).

Fiesta of «Pero Palo.»

Villanueva de la Vera, Cáceres province. Ancient tradition. *Pero Palo* is a puppet representing the devil. Young men carry it around the town on their shoulders and then, dancing around it to the music of drums, impale and decapitate it. Drums rolling, the puppet is carried on a wheelbarrow to a tomb where it is buried, and afterwards a huge banquet is held and a flag of Arabian origin is hoisted to preside over the festivities.

Carnival in Cádiz.

Cádiz. Dating from very remote times. Consisting of a cavalcade, contests to choose the best chorus and joke-teller (where a type of humor peculiar to Cádiz has its heyday), masquerade balls, election of the queen of the fiesta, and fireworks.

«Fallas» of San José.

Valencia. Their origin goes back to the Middle Ages, but they did not acquire their current form until the mid-19th century. A triumph of popular art, the *fallas* (huge cardboard or papier mâché figures) and *ninots* (cardboard dolls) express, as in no other way, the gay, satiric spirit of the Valencian people. Among the many acts held throughout the two weeks of festivities, with outsiders and natives of the city taking part in the gaity, especially noteworthy are the *Cridá,* the proclamation read from the Torres de Serranos by the young woman chosen «Miss Fallera» and the mayor of the city; the *Ninot* Cavalcade, a humorous nighttime procession in which several fiesta committees take part, forming what might be called «living *fallas*»; the Cavalcade of the Kingdom, in which people from several towns of the ancient Kingdom of Valencia take part, with their own typical folklore and attire; the offering of flowers by women participants in the festivities to Nuestra Señora de los Desamparados (the city's Patron Saint), and above all the *Nit del Foc* («Night of Fire») whose high point is the fascinating and awesome *Cremá* when all the *fallas* are set on fire. Other major fiesta events are the bullfights and sports competitions.

Fiestas of Mary Magdalene.

Castellón de la Plana. Third Sunday of Lent. Dating back to the 15th century, they acquired even greater impulse after 1945. Major events include a picturesque cavalcade, a procession in which the festivities are officially proclaimed; the outing to the hermitage of Saint Mary Magdalene, the nighttime procession of «The Return,» with the carved image of the *Crucificado de la Purísima Sangre,* and the parade of the *gayatas,* colorfully illuminated staves and poles.

Cherry Fiestas.

Community of the Valle del Jerte, Cáceres province. Celebrated by the visit of members of the region's cooperatives and brotherhoods to the Jerte Valley, with literary and choral contests.

«La Passió».

Esparraguera, Barcelona province. A survival of the Mystery and Miracle plays of medieval European theater, the Passion of Christ has been performed in this town since the 16th century. Amateurs from the town direct and perform in it, and at times the same personage is passed from father to son. Performances are held at the Gran Teatro de la Passió, a modern building specifically constructed for Passion plays. It is divided into two parts and 48 scenes: the first, the Public Life and Passion of Christ, and the second, Death and Resurrection, performed in the morning and afternoon respectively.

Sacred Drama of «La Passió».

Uldecona, Tarragona province. The text of this sacred drama dates from the 16th century and consists of three in-quarto folios, of two columns each, in verse form.

SPRING

«Mercat del Ram».

Vich, Barcelona province. Dating from the Middle Ages. A variety of popular festivities, including the election of the Queen of the Fiestas. There are also special contests such as outdoor painting, photography, amateur film-making, store fronts and stands, as well as practical demonstrations in the Agricultural and Cattle-raising pavillions.

Fiesta of the Sweetcake.

Avilés, Oviedo province. A wide variety of festivities ranging from a carriage parade in honor of the Queen of the Fiestas and her ladies-in-waiting to a cattle show and contest, including as well regattas on the river and performances by folkloric groups.

Fiesta of the Painted Eggs.

Pola de Siero, Oviedo province. Very remote origin. Formerly, the eggs were cooked in soot, giving them a rough appearance; they are now painted with aniline dyes of a hundred different colors, and are true works of artisanship. During the fiesta they are sold by the thousand. A huge folkloric parade is held in the afternoon: groups from nearly all the town councils of Asturias parade through the town, each performing a typical dance when passing by the Town Hall Square.

Edict of the Orchard.

Murcia. Popular folkloric cavalcade with the orchard as the main theme, with carriages, serenaders and groups of regional dancers, participants wearing regional costumes, and wagons decorated in countryside fashion. Booths with products and wine from the province of Murcia installed in the city.

Battle of Flowers.

Murcia. Battle of flowers held in an enclosed area with a cavalcade of carriages, bands of music and majorettes.

Burial of the Sardine.

Murcia. Nighttime festivity at the end of the Spring Fiestas. Twenty-five carriages participate, with masqueraders, groups of torchbearers, bands of music. Thousands of toys are thrown to spectators from the carriages. At the end of the festivity, the «Sardine» is set on fire and fireworks are set off.

«La Folia».

San Vicente de la Barquera, Santander province. These festivities in honor of the town's Patron Saint, dating back to medieval times, begin with lively reveilles, followed by a folkloric parade to the parish church, and end with the procession of the Virgin, carried by seamen on their shoulders to an altar located on the wharf of the harbor—where popular dances are performed—and later taken by sea to a sanctuary. Those interested in attending this fiesta should consult the Town Hall to confirm the date it is to be held.

Moors and Christians.

Alcoy, Alicante province. First celebrated in the 17th century. Participants dressed as Moors and Christians dance through the streets to the rhythm of the strident music played by bands. A battle is then enacted whose highest points are the deployment of the warriors, the embassy mission of the Arabs, the harquebus battle, the embassy mission of the Christians and the final battle, with the victory of the Crusaders, who shoot arrows at the defeated Arabs in flight, amid the piercing noise of firecrackers and ringing church bells.

St. George's Day and the Book Fair.

Barcelona. Since the year 1714, the people of Barcelona have celebrated the custom of visiting the chapel of St. George at the Town Council to pray before the saint's image. The same day (the equivalent of St. Valentine's Day) stands selling roses are set up in the patio and around the building of the Town Council, while countless book stalls are set up in the squares and strategic points of the city, as «Book Day» is celebrated on the same date (coinciding with the anniversary of the death of Cervantes). It is also the custom to give a rose and a book to one's most cherished friends.

April Fair.

Seville. In little more than a century, Seville's April Fairs, originally livestock markets, have become one of Spain's most fascinating spectacles. Morning, noon and night, the Fairground is a lively sight with its multicolored stalls, garlands and paper lanterns, although the high points in the day are the noon promenade of horseback riders and the singing and dancing in the wee hours when «magic» comes to the throats of the flamenco singers and to the arms and legs of the dancers. Horses are ridden by couples dressed in Andalusian style: ruffled shirts, chaps and wide-brim hats; gaily garlanded carriages are pulled by draft horses with bells jangling from their harnesses. During Fair time the lovely city of Seville is transformed: gaiety is the dominant note and the dancing and singing and drinking carry on non-stop. Excellent bullfights, held in the Maestranza ring—the bullfight «cathedral»—, complete the festivities.

Outing of the Virgen de la Cabeza.

Andújar, Jaén province. The fiestas begin with saddle and quarter horse competitions held in the bull ring, with Andalusia's top horsemen taking part. On the afternoon of the second day of the fiesta, a reception is held for the over fifty brotherhoods that come from all over Spain. The Sanctuary of the Virgen de la Cabeza is located on the highest mountain of the Sierra Morena: after congregating in Andújar, on the third day of the fiesta, thousands of excursionists, or *romeros,* from all over the region, dressed in Andalusian style and mounted on many different types of horses, climb up to the Sanctuary. At night, they sing and dance and set off firecrackers outside the Sanctuary, while other *romeros* prostrate themselves before the Virgin. On the last day of the fiesta, the Virgin is carried in a procession, and upon their return to Andújar, the excursionists continue their merrymaking late into the night.

Fair and Exhibit in Honour of the Wine of the Ribeiro Region.

Ribadavia, Orense province. Several typical celebrations are held in honor of the region's famous wines which, along with regional dishes, visitors are invited to taste. Music and dance of the area add a note of gaiety to the festivities.

Olive Fiesta.

Mora de Toledo, Toledo province. Celebrated since 1947 to mark the end of the olive harvest. Large parade of carriages, garlanded wagons, serenading and folkloric groups. Exhibit of crafts, livestock and olive-derived products.

National Festival of Spring Songs.

Alcázar de San Juan, Ciudad Real province. The fiesta consists of folkloric groups dressed in traditional costumes that sing May Day songs and serenades.

Cartagena. (Holy Week).

Murcia province. Processions were first held here in the 16th century, and still conserve their ancient mood and atmosphere. Two large and venerable religious brotherhoods—the *Californios* and the *Marrajos*—polarize the devotion of the faithful.

Cuenca. (Holy Week).

Soberly adorned and beautiful religious images mounted on platforms are carried by penitants in grave silence—interrupted only by the clarions of the tubas—through the ancient part of the city, awesomely perched on high cliffs. Simultaneously in the Church of San Miguel the Week of Religious Music is held, with renowned performers taking part. Each year a new work by an eminent composer is premiered, and the «Tomás Luis de Vitoria» Music Composition Prize is awarded.

Granada. (Holy Week).

Holy Week here is characterized above all by the awesome beauty of the religious images, works of the great masters of this art such as Diego de Siloé, Pablo de Rojas, Alonso Cano, Martínez Montañés, Pedro de Mena and José de Mora; by the exquisite taste of the images' adornments; and, finally, by the enchanting and mysterious sites where the images are carried in procession through this city, influenced as no other by Arabian culture.

Híjar. (Holy Week).

Teruel province. Lovely processions with the odd feature of the deafening roll of hundreds of drums and the indefatigable beating of countless brass drums, which all gets off to a frenzied start on the stroke of midnight on Thursday in the town square.

Lorca. (Holy Week).

Murcia province. Its festivities are very original, consisting of a lovely parade of over 100 legendary and historical personages from antiquity, held on Friday.

Málaga. (Holy Week).

On monumental baroque thrones, borne by the so-called «throne men,» superb religious images are carried in procession (the works of Pedro de Mena, Valdivieso, Zayas and Benlliure, to cite the greatest masters), while those of the Virgin are covered with sumptuous cloaks embroidered in silver and gold. Renowned painters such as Moreno Carbonero and Sallaverría decorated the banners of some of the thirty brotherhoods that take part in the procession. Especially lovely is the procession of the Virgen de los Dolores, whose image is borne through the streets after midnight on Friday, illuminated only by the light of the was candles carried by penitants.

Moncada. (Holy Week).

Valencia province. The Mistery Play of the Passion is a realistic enactment of the Passion of Christ, held in stages all through Holy Week. The crucifixion takes place on the hill of Santa Bárbara, where there is a hermitage which is the starting point of a procession on Friday after the Death of Christ has been enacted.

Murcia. (Holy Week).

Here the beautiful images sculpted by Salzillo, so different from those of Castile and Andalusia, are carried in processions through the city. On Thursday afternoon in front of the Church of Jesus, the *Auroros* sing in five voices ancient songs of Murcia allusive to the Passion of Christ.

Pollensa. (Holy Week).

Island of Mallorca. On Good Friday the *Devallement* is held, whose origin dates back to the Middle Ages: at night, in the midst of absolute silence, townspeople, wearing the typical cape of the area and lit only by torchlight, carry down the image of the Lying Christ from the Oratorio del Calvario, located on the hill overlooking the town, to the parish Church of Nuestra Señora de los Angeles.

Seville. (Holy Week).

In the capital of Andalusia, Holy Week celebrations reach unbelievable religious and aesthetic heights. Over 60 brotherhoods participate in the processions following an official itinerary that begins at the popular Campana Square, continues along the typical Sierpes Street, passes in front of the plateresque Town Hall and, after going through the Gothic Cathedral, ends at the Giralda tower and baroque Archbishop's Palace. The images, silver or carved wood, covered with carnations—and those of the Virgins with sumptuous mantles—rock slightly on the shoulders of their porters while *saetas* (religious songs sung in processions) are heard. The images are the work of renowned artists such as Roldán, Juan de Mena and Martínez Montañés.

Valencia. (Holy Week).

The typical and strange processions of the maritime neighborhoods are especially interesting for their variety and colorfulness. The main feature of the processions are the biblical personages enacted by members—altogether over 2,000 people—of 21 religious brotherhoods and associations. Especially noteworthy is the Resurrection Procession.

Vergés. (Holy Week).

Gerona province. From ten to twelve on the night of Holy Thursday, this town holds an unusual procession: in a rectangular plaza, at the foot of the towers of the town's ancient walls, several scenes from the Life and Passion of Christ are enacted, from the conversion of the Samaritans to the moment in which Jesus carries the cross. Then the man playing Christ carries his cross to the parish church where a group representing evangelists, followed by others carrying images, await him, and they return by the same route back to the point of departure. Twice during the procession a very ancient dance—the *Dança de la mort* or «Dance of Death»—is performed.

Zamora. (Holy Week).

Thirteen religious brotherhoods carrying 34 images (the best of which are the austere Castilian scenes) take part in this awesomely ascetic and fervent procession. On Easter Sunday all the townspeople go to the Plaza Mayor where shotguns are fired from the balconies in celebration.

Outing to the Trasona Dam.

Corvera de Asturias, Oviedo province. Recently created by the workers of Ensidesa, it includes festivities of Asturian folklore, contests of clog makers and other artisans as well as sports competitions.

Fiestas of Santísima Vera Cruz.

Caravaca de la Cruz, Murcia province. Medieval origin. Especially interesting is the ancient ceremony which consists of placing the Vera Cruz in a silver jar filled with wine, which then spills over onto the flowers set around it and these are later handed out to the faithful; the race of the «wine horses» in which young men run dizzily among the galloping riderless horses; the parley between Christian and Moorish kings, and finally the blessing of the waterways that irrigate the fields by immersing a cross in them.

Festival of the Patios of Córdoba.

Córdoba. Dating back many years. It includes the outing of the Virgen Conquistadora over the sierra to the Linares Sanctuary with richly adorned carriages and riders; May Day contests of patios, gratings and balconies with all the patios, streets and most typical squares adorned with flowers; and an important flamenco contest held every three years (the ninth contest held in 1980) in which amateur performers participate in the dance, song and guitar recitals.

Horse Fair.

Jerez de la Frontera, Cádiz province. Of ancient origin (1284), it was at first a livestock market and through the centuries evolved into what is now a sum of festivities that can be grouped as follows: 1. Select Livestock Market and Exhibit, and Fair and Exhibit of Agricultural and Industrial Machinery; 2. Popular celebrations including bullfights, typical dances and songs in the fair stalls set up in the González-Hontoria park; 3. The Horse Fair as such with saddle and harness horse competitions and a horse market and exhibit.

Patron Saint Fiestas of Santo Domingo.

Santo Domingo de la Calzada, Logroño province. The first day of fiestas includes a sheep parade with two colorfully decorated sheep that will later be sacrificed for the Saint's meal; the so-called procession of branches in which oxen pull wagons filled with branches of holm oak to adorn Santo Domingo's tomb, and the procession of prioresses in which women and female family members of men who were priors of the brotherhood wear basket hats with veils. On the second day, several processions are held, including that of the Saint's bread, the pilgrim and the maidens, and that of the wheel in which a gaily adorned wheel is carried by the townspeople on their shoulders and then lifted by ropes to the dome of the cathedral in front of the Saint's tomb. On the Patron Saint's day the above-mentioned meal is served and a solemn procession is held.

Hispano-Arabic Fiestas in Honor of San Bonifacio.

Petrel, Alicante province. These fiestas date back two hundred and fifty years. Some 2,100 masqueraders participate, in ten groups, five from the Moorish band—«Old Moors,» «Moroccans,» «Bedouins,» «Border Moors,» «Berbers»—and five from the Christian band—«Troops from Flanders,» «Seamen,» «Students,» «Plowmen,» «Biscayans»—.Each group has a captain, a *rodela*—a four-year-old girl—and a standard-bearer—a young woman under twenty years of age—. The celebration is divided into the following acts: retreat with firework castles, entry of Christians, entry of Moors, descent of the Saint from the hermitage, two embassy parleys, procession, raising of the Saint to the hermitage and designation of *rodelas* and standard-bearers for the following year.

Rocío Outing.

Almonte, Huelva province. Very ancient origin. Countless wagons pulled by oxen and decked out in flowers and wax adornments, come from Huelva, Cádiz and Seville, as well as hundreds of riders with young women seated on their horses' croups, all dressed in Andalusian style. They make their way through the countryside to the sound of the flute and the timbrel as they head for the Sanctuary of Nuestra Señora del Rocío. Once there, they take part in religious ceremonies such as the nighttime rosary in which the faithful walk through the marshlands holding candles, or the procession in which the young men carry the Virgin on their shoulders. Flamenco songs and dances–*seguiriyas* and *sevillanas rocieras*–continue non-stop throughout the fiesta.

The Cavalcade.

Atienza, Guadalajara province. This fiesta commemorates an historical event that took place in 1162 when the muleteers of Atienza liberated King Alphonse VIII from falling into the hands of his uncle Ferdinand II of León who wanted to remove him from the throne. The members of the brotherhood, riding mules and wearing long capes and black hats, go through the town preceded by bagpipe players, a standard-bearer, the abbot, the steward of the brotherhood, six choir boys and the major-domo. They make their way to the Estrella hermitage where they hear mass which is followed by a procession and a meal offered by the brotherhood; the retinue returns in the afternoon and again parades through the town. The members of the brotherhood then compete in furious races on the outskirts of Puerta Caballo and, at the end of the day, elect a new head brother in front of the Church of the Trinidad.

«Fiesta Mayor».

San Feliu de Pallarois, Gerona province. First celebrated in the 8th century. It includes performances of archaic dances–*Els caballets*–with characters such as a pair of giants and a *mulassa* (a cardboard and cloth mule carried by two or three men).

Sardana Fest.

Calella, Barcelona province. The country's major sardana *cum* folklore celebration, it is held in the town's Municipal Park, with the participation of Catalonia's best sardana dancers and orchestras.

Fiestas of San Juan del Monte.

Miranda de Ebro, Burgos province. A long parade of colorfully dressed quadrilles playing

different instruments files through the town, singing, dancing and waving their round caps. This is followed by an outing to the Saint's hermitage which lies some five kilometers away with participants either going on foot and dancing as they go or in handsomely adorned carriages.

The «Patum».

Berga, Barcelona province. This is a very ancient drama with a mixture of religious and secular themes, enacted in mime and dance in the San Pedro Square, in front of the Casa de la Ciudad. It consists of six scenes, all of them reflecting typical or amusing manners and customs.

Bonfire of San Juan.

Alicante. The «bonfires», in reality true artistic monuments made of wood, cardboard and cloth representing figures that satirize people's bad habits, are constructed during the so-called *plantá* and are burned three days later (in the meantime the whole town goes out to see them) in the ceremony called the *Cremá*. Four cavalcades go through the city: the *Foc Cavalcade,* representing the cult of fire in different epochs; the *Coso Infantil* in which young boys and girls dress up in disguises; the *Coso Multicolor* in which flowers, confetti and streamers are strewn in the streets, and the bands of music (hired by the festival commissions) that parade through the streets. A folklore exhibit is also held in which samples from different areas of the province are displayed. Other important acts include a castle and fireworks contest, a bull fair, and various religious acts such as the flower offering to the Virgen del Remedio, Patron Saint and Mayoress of the city.

Fiestas of San Juan.

Ciudadela, Island of Menorca. Celebrated since the 14th century. On Sunday, the *Junta de Caixers,* presided by the *S'Homo dés Be* who walks barefooted covered in animal pelts and carrying a sheep (representing San Juan), goes through the town inviting the people to the fiesta. During the vigil of San Juan, an outing to the Saint's hermitage is held. Mounted participants—dressed up in short pants, riding boots, vests, tails, a pointed hat, and a sword at their belts—caracole their horses in the city's main square. On the Day of San Juan, the riders take part in lively medieval jousts: the game of the embrace, in which two riders try to join together on the same horse at a full gallop; the masqueraders' game in which clay balls are hurled, etc.

Passage of Fire and Fiesta of the «Móndidas».

San Pedro Manrique, Soria province. Dating back to time immemorial. The men of the town, generally carrying another person on their shoulders, cross over a carpet of live coals barefooted. The *móndidas*—women with basket bonnets and shrubs, dressed in white (according to some versions, they represent the priestesses of ancient Celtiberian tribes)—hold a procession, and the leader offers the first shrub to the priest.

Fiestas of San Juan.

Coria, Cáceres province. Every day, in the morning and at night, a bull is let loose in the ancient area of this walled city where it is shut in by four large doors. It is left to roam in the old part of the town for two or three hours, until the fiesta's standard-bearer gives the order for it to be killed. During these hours, townspeople dance and sing in the streets and visit *Peñas* where they drink the typical fiesta punch. Then, when the bull appears, everyone runs to safety. Among Spain's bull fiestas, this one is quite unique.

Dances of the Corpus Octave.

Valverde de los Arroyos, Guadalajara province. They date from the 16th century. Dancers, eight plus the *Botarga* and the flute-and-drum player, surround the Holy Sacrament and dance to lovely ancient folkloric tunes.

Outing of San Felices de Bilbio.

Haro, Logroño province. The fiestas in honor of San Felices de Bilbio, the Patron Saint of Haro, begin with several religious acts. An outing to the cliffs of Bilbio (where there is a hermitage) is organized and, after mass and adoration of the relics, a wine battle is held in which young men spout wine at each other from their gourds.

Fiestas of San Juan de la Madre de Dios.

Soria. Celebrated since the 13th century. These festivities hark back to the time when the entire city, divided into twelve quadrilles, celebrated the brotherhood of the five days, with their typical denominations: Thursday, *la saca* or selection of the bulls; Friday, *de toros,* the major bullfight day; Saturday, *agés*; Sunday, *de calderas,* when the cooked meat of the bulls is distributed among the townspeople; and Monday, *de bailas,* the last day of the fiesta in which multitudinous dances are held. Typical bull runs are also held, as well as outings and free bullfights.

Fiesta of San Pedro.

Lequeitio, Vizcaya province. The main attraction of these ancient fiestas is the *Kaxarranca:* a man carried on a raised platform by eight young men. Wearing a black frock coat and white pants, carrying the flag of San Pedro in one hand and a top hat in the other, he dances in his stocking feet to the sound of the *txistu* (Basque instrument) and the timbrel.

The «Amuravela».

Cudillero, Oviedo province. Held since the 16th century. The events of the year, partly religious and partly humorous, are narrated in verse and in *pixueto* (dialect spoken in Cudillero) in front of the image of San Pedro which is carried in procession to the sea shore.

Muster of San Marcial.

Irún, Guipúzcoa province. To commemorate the battle of San Marcial, the *Alarde* or muster—twelve companies, with torchbearers and cavalry, consisting of some 2,000 men—go to the hermitage of San Marcial on this Saint's Day. After mass, a lively outing is held. Parades and popular entertainment complete the list of festivities.

Lustral Fiestas of the Lowering of the Virgin.

Santa Cruz de la Palma, Santa Cruz de Tenerife province. Held every five years since 1676, they consist of archaic theatrical performances in a huge coach with sumptuous stage scenery (the allegoric triumphal carriage), in a dry-stone nave located in the Nieves gorge (the dialogue between the castle and the nave) and in public squares (dances of dwarves and short dramatic poems). It was last held in 1980.

Thursday of the Octave of Corpus Christi.

Villa de La Orotava, Santa Cruz de Tenerife province. Originated in the 19th century. The most solemn act of these fiestas consists of the preparation of carpets of natural flowers spread out in the streets of the monumental area of town and in the square of the Town Hall where an artistic carpet is made with different colors of the earth from the world renowned Cañadas del Teide. In the center of the square the Holy Sacrament is placed in a silver throne.

Outing of San Isidro Labrador.

Villa de la Orotava, Santa Cruz de Tenerife province. It consists of a parade of the faithful who carry images of the town's Patron Saints, San Isidro and Santa María de la Cabeza, on raised platforms. Amid the typical music and song of this excursion—*ajijides*—, they make symbolic offerings of fruit and earth to the Saints. Excursionists use wagons and carriages—reflecting the agricultural life of the area—in the pilgrimage, and large crowds of merrymakers gather to sing popular and folk-loric songs.

Puenteareas.

Pontevedra province. Special interest is given to the procession by the lovely carpets of leafless natural flowers—a prodigious show of popular art—covering the streets where the Holy Sacrament is carried.

Sitges.

Barcelona province. Since 1950 this celebration has been characterized by the amazing artistic floral carpets spread throughout the town. In the center of the main square, packed with flowers, an altar rises from which the blessing with the Holy Sacrament is celebrated while carnations are virtually showered into the air. The same day the National Carnation Show is held and several thousand pots from different countries are on display.

Toledo.

Presided by the Primate of Spain, the very solemn procession of the Corpus, with the magnificent monstrance designed by Arfe, takes place amid the fervor of the faithful and the uncomparable framework of one of Spain's most beautiful and mysterious cities. Medieval life is evoked in the gowns worn by the different participants: the red habits of the Royal Brotherhood of Infanzones de Illescas; the blue habits of the Mozarabic Knights; the white habits of the Knights of the Holy Sepulcher, and the green gowns of the Knights of Corpus Christi.

Dancers and Sins.

Camuñas, Toledo province. Spectacular medieval dances include a mime enactment of a short religious play in which grace triumphs over sin. The actors' costumes are sumptuous and amazingly fanciful.

Octave of Corpus Christi.

Peñalsordo, Badajoz province. Sunday following Corpus Christi. Celebrated since the 16th century. It includes a simulacrum of a battle against the Arabs and the construction of a human castle. In thanksgiving for the victory in battle, the Holy Sacrament is worshiped with the accompaniment of castanets, cowbells and drums.

SUMMER

«Rapa das Bestas».

San Lorenzo de Sabucedo-La Estrada, Pontevedra province. Dating from the 16th century. At dawn, young men go to the mountain to round up the wild horses that roam there and take them to the parish church; the following morning, in the stone-walled «ring» of the parish atrium, the horses are mounted one by one by those who will later cut their manes. Two days later before dawn, the horses are again set loose at the foot of the mountain.

«Rapa das Bestas».

Vivero, Lugo province. Before dawn the «mounters» round up the horses of different municipal districts and take them to San Andrés de Boimonte where the animals are enclosed in a so-called *curro*. Then the *rapa* begins: the horses' manes and tails are cut and colts are branded, and afterwards they are let loose again in the mountains. Participants are invited to a typical garlic soup.

Fiestas of San Fermín.

Pamplona. The exact date when these world-famous fiestas were first held is not known, however, documents show that they existed at least as far back as 1591. They begin when the president of the Fiesta Commission sets off an explosion of fireworks from the balcony of the Town Hall. Then bands of music, *txistu* and bagpipe players make their way through the city to the outskirts playing lively reveilles to announce the bull run of the bulls that will be fought that afternoon. The *encierros* or bull runs are the most exciting part of the fiestas: young men from Pamplona, and many foreigners as well, decked out in typical garb, run—at great risk—in front of the bulls that are set loose in the streets as far as the bull ring where the animals will later be used in the bullfights. Day and night, without stop, groups of young people make their way through the city singing and dancing and drinking. Other notes of festivity are added by the fireworks, livestock fairs and the presence of over a hundred *txistu* players belonging to the Basque-Navarre Association.

Fiestas of «Coso Blanco».

Castro Urdiales, Santander province. Dating from 1948. Especially noteworthy is the flower battle and the nighttime parade of carriages preceded by a fireworks display.

Sardana Fest.

Olot, Gerona province. From early in the morning to late at night, numerous *collas*—some including groups from France—dance sardanas to the rhythm of the music played by the region's best instrumentalists.

Fiestas of San Benitiño de Lérez.

Pontevedra. The outing to the sanctuary begins at dawn, and at noon the procession of the Saint departs, carrying an image representing a young boy in abbot's clothing holding a miter and a staff; then a huge country-style meal is held, with the background music of bagpipes and Galician songs. The festivities end with typical choruses and dances. This fiesta coincides with the celebration of the Galician Song Festival.

Fiestas of the Virgen del Carmen.

San Pedro del Pinatar, Murcia province. Very ancient origin. In the morning seamen carry the image of the Virgin on their shoulders to the Mar Menor where it is put on a boat which, escorted by many others, heads for Lo Pagán. There the image is taken from the boat and placed on an altar facing the sea. Mass is held, attended by the faithful from their boats. Following different sports contests, the return is announced at eleven p.m. by a lavish display of fireworks.

Stilt Dances.

Anguiano, Logroño province. Very remote origin. Within the Patron Saint fiestas of Saint Mary Magdalene, eight young men decked out in multicolored blouses and skirts and wearing 40-centimeter-high stilts accompany the procession of the Saint, dancing to the sound of bagpipes and timbrels and playing castanets.

Traditional Fiestas of Santa Cristina.

Lloret de Mar, Gerona province. In the morning the Saint's image is carried in procession to the beach where it is embarked on a handsomely adorned fishing boat which carries it by sea to its hermitage. Other boats follow carrying local authorities, clergymen, provosts, musicians and crowds of excursionists. In the afternoon in the main square of the town of Lloret, an ancient dance called *ses morratxes,* possibly of Arabian origin, is performed. The dance is repeated two days later.

Fiesta of the Shepherd.

Cangas de Onís, Oviedo province. First celebrated in 1939. Its objective is to honor the

shepherds of the National Park of the Mountain of Covadonga, and is held in the Vega de Enol beside the lake of the same name. The fiesta begins in the morning with mass, after which an open session is held at the Town Hall and shepherds take part in electing the Councilman of Pastures, while other matters of interest to shepherds are also discussed. Afterwards shepherds take part in a number of sports contests while choral groups and dancers liven up the festivity with regional songs and dances.

Moors and Christians in Honor of Saint Martha.

Villajoyosa, Alicante province. These festivities differ from other similar fiestas of Levante in that the battles between Moors and Christians take place not only on land but on sea as well. On the main day of the fiestas, just as the sun begins to rise, the entire town goes to the beach to watch the confrontations between Christian and Moorish ships. The latter win and the battle continues on the beach with the Saracens taking the city. At the end of the day, the Christians, now recovered, throw the invading forces out to sea, and the image of Saint Martha is carried in a triumphal procession throughout the streets of Villajoyosa.

Fiesta of the «Vaqueiros» of Alzada.

Luarca, Oviedo province. This festivity is celebrated in the Braña de Aristébano (a summer pastureland) which belongs to the town council of Luarca. The folkloric groups within the pastureland district of the town council take part in the fiesta bringing with them the region's classic instruments: the *pandeiro*, castanets and the *payetsa* (a pan with a very long handle beaten with an iron key to keep time to the music). A *boda vaqueria* («cowboy wedding») is held during the fiesta: the fiancés and guests go to the chapel from the bride's house, all of them riding on horseback and wearing regional costumes. Huge country-style meal. Performances of dances, popular ballads and songs. Election of a cowboy couple and cowgirl queen. To attend the festivities men must wear the typical peaked cap, and women the Asturian skirt. Only bagpipe music is allowed.

Medieval Theater Festival.

Hita, Guadalajara province. In the morning a falconry contest is held, in the late afternoon tournaments begin and, at night, in the main square of the town, a medieval play based on the works of the Archbishop of Hita is enacted. The last act portrays the battle between *Don* Carnal and *Doña* Lent, in which *Don* Love is the victor. This is followed by a parade of masqueraders, musicians, dancers and *botargas*, or masked men jangling cowbells.

Patron Saint Fiestas in Honor of San Lorenzo.

Foz, Lugo province. Noteworthy are the seamen's procession of the Saint, regional dance contests and sports competitions.

Official Fiestas.

Estella, Navarre province. Medieval origin. Groups of young men live it up in the streets of the town with a great deal of fanfare. *Encierros,* or bull runs (with young bulls). The solemn procession of San Andrés is announced by giant cardboard figures and *shepes,* or cardboard horses without legs held at the waist by suspenders. The fiesta ends with the *abadeja,* an open-air meal consisting of a dish prepared with garlic and peppers, served by the young men of the town.

Canoe Fiesta of Asturias.

Arriondas-Ribadesella, Oviedo province. At eleven a.m. the canoeists' parade begins in Arriondas. They are grouped by nationality and each group is accompanied by one of the fiesta Misses. The race begins at the bridge over the Sella River in Arriondas and finishes 18 kilometers downstream at the Ribadesella bridge. People follow the race from cars and trains, stopping at strategic points to watch the canoeists pass. The fiesta ends with an excursion to the countryside of Ova.

Fiestas in Honor of Nuestra Señora de las Nieves.

Villa de Agaete, Canary Islands, Las Palmas province. The main activities include the lowering of the branch, the offering of the excursionists to the image of the Virgin and the lowering of the Virgin.

Patron Saint Fiestas of the White Virgin.

Vitoria. 19th-century origin. On the first day of the fiestas at six p.m., the mayor sets off fireworks from the main balcony of the Town Hall and, at the same time, the flags of Spain and Vitoria are raised, bands of music begin to play and the descent of the mythical *Celedón* from the tower of San Miguel to the main square, packed with crowds, begins. Half an hour later, town hall officials, preceded by bands of music, *txistu* players and groups of dancers, go to the Church of San Miguel to attend the solemn vespers in honor of the White Virgin. At nine p.m. the traditional procession of the rosary or of the lanterns is held. On the following days, townspeople wear the image of the Virgin on their blouses, while bullfights and parades of huge cardboard figures add to the general atmosphere of merrymaking. On the last night, after a huge string of firecrackers has been set off, *Celedón* descends through the air to his tower while bands of music play full blast and the crowds wave handkerchiefs.

Albariño Wine Fiesta.

Cambados, Pontevedra province. The central attraction of this fiesta are the wine-tasting sessions in which the region's best wines are given awards. Popular festivities and sports events complete the agenda.

Fiesta of Santa Cruz.

Ribadeo, Lugo province. During a festive outing to the Santa Cruz Mountain, regional music in its purest form is played outside an ancient hermitage, the Monument to the Galician Bagpipe Player and the Cross of Light. Contests of bagpipe quartets and quintets are also held.

Day of Asturias.

Gijón, Oviedo province. The regional importance of this fiesta is witnessed by the fact that all the mayors of Asturias attend the festivity as guests of honor. The main attraction consists of a pompous and spectacular parade of carriages decorated by regional and foreign folkloric groups and which ends in a multitudinous typical outing to the countryside.

Mystery Play of Elche.

Elche, Alicante province. Enacted since the 13th century, and declared a National Artistic Monument in 1931. This extraordinary sacred drama, unique living example of primitive lyric theater, is also unique in that it is the only one in the world held inside a church—the Basilica of Santa María—thanks to a special privilege granted it by Pope Urbano VIII. Divided into two acts, the first enacts the death of the Virgin, attended by apostles and angels, and the second shows the Assumption of Our Lady to heaven. The Mystery Play of Elche is a beautiful and moving spectacle, with its exquisite archaic music, its audacious stage machinery, its excellent actors. Not often does religious feeling find such a close ally in aesthetic intuition and artistic splendor and with such purity as in this Mystery Play.

Fiestas of the Traditions of San Roque.

Garachico, Santa Cruz de Tenerife. Its origin goes back to the 17th century. The Sunday before the Day of San Roque, the so-called «Fiesta of the Traditions» is held to honor vernacular customs with the participation of poets, orators and folkloric groups, and the election of the Miss of the Fiesta. On the Day of San Ro-que an outing to the Saint's hermitage is held, with wagons and horses gaily adorned. Serenading and an excursion to the seaside follows, and the fiesta ends with a display of fireworks.

Mystery Play of San Guillén and Santa Felicia.

Obanos, Navarre province. A sacred drama, premiered in 1965. Enacted in the main town square by over 600 participants. Against the background of medieval pilgrimages to Compostela, the drama narrates the martyrdom of Felicia by her brother Guillén de Aquitania, the latter's repentance and the miraculous apparition of the Virgen de Arnotegui.

International Descent from Pisuerga and Palencia's Canoe Fiesta.

Alar del Rey, Palencia province. A large number of canoeists take part in this competition which begins at Olleros del Pisuerga and ends at the bridge of the Monjas of Alar del Rey where there is a plaque commemorating the descent on which the winners' names are engraved. Large crowds turn out for the competition which they watch from cars and trains.

Mountain Day.

Cabezón de la Sal, Santander province. Folkloric fiestas with contests of whistle players, tambourines, rebecs, mountain songs, rope throwing and cattle roping.

Octopus Fiesta.

Carballino, Orense province. Folkloric and gastronomic fiesta with the participation of choral groups, and a huge meal with octopus as the main dish. Bagpipe players add to the merriment.

Fiestas of San Roque.

Betanzos, La Coruña province. They date from the 15th century. Aside from the guild dances of peasants and seamen performed during the votive offering and procession of the Saint, these fiestas include a country outing to Los Caneiros in boats down the Mandeo River which engage in a flower battle at night; the setting in flight of a huge balloon and, on the Day of San Roque, a major fair.

Fiestas of the Assumption («La Loa»).

La Alberca, Salamanca province. Dating back to remote times, it is held outside the church

atrium and is similar to a religious play. On the day of the Assumption the offering to Virgin by the Major-domo in the main square is held. It is attended by people from the surrounding mountain villages dressed up in their best traditional costumes. The next day the *Loa* is enacted, consisting of a speech recited by the «comic» who sings the first part and then ends with words of praise for the Virgin recited by the «clown» and the «courtiers.»

«Fiesta Mayor.»

Amer, Gerona province. The main attraction is the so-called mayor's sardana or *batlle* which is held in the main square. A sardana is danced—sometimes composed exclusively for this solemn occasion—which was chosen by the mayor when he took office and which is only played on this occasion. This sardana is the only one danced in a large circle, thus allowing any and all to participate.

Patron Saint Fiestas of San Roque.

Sada, La Coruña province. In spite of its other festivities—raising of a giant paper balloon, rowboat regatta, parade of carriages with flower battles—, the biggest draw to outsiders is the *sardiñada*: at stands set up by seamen, participants are invited to eat grilled sardines, *cachelos* (typical Galician dish of meat or fish with potatoes), corn bread and wine.

Floral Gala.

Torrelavega, Santander province. First celebrated in 1956, it centers on a showy and spectacular artistic contest of carriages, with a parade of folkloric and musical associations and a flower battle.

Patron Saint Fiestas of San Bartolomé Apóstol.

Tarazona de la Mancha, Albacete province. They reach their high point on the Day of San Bartolomé, and include bullfights, sports competitions and gay popular festivities. Festivals of Spain. Parades of carriages and masqueraders. Opening of the Fair.

Fairs and Fiestas of the Wine Harvest.

Requena, Valencia province. Inaugurated by public proclamation in which townspeople on foot and on horseback, dressed up in old-fashioned garb and preceded by drums and trumpets, parade through the streets. The most noteworthy act is the inauguration with the burning of an allegoric monument to the wine harvest where a fountain is installed from which wine flows freely and everyone is invited to drink.

Flower Battle.

Laredo, Santander province. Held since 1908 in the town's main street, flanked by a tribune, prizes are given to the most lavishly decorated carriages.

Fiestas of Moors and Christians.

Onteniente, Valencia province. The confrontation between Moors and Christians is similar to others held in Levante, all celebrated in a mood of humor and gaiety.

Fiesta of the «Regalina».

Cadaveo-Luarca, Oviedo province. Parade of adorned wagons accompanied by bagpipe players and drummers, groups of regional dancers and people carrying *anfiladas* (biscuits made from wheat flour, eggs, lard, yeast and sugar). During the parade a public proclamation is read in verse in the dialect of Cadaveo by the crier of the *Regalina* Fiesta. The parade then goes to the excursion grounds, next to the hermitage of the Virgin, where the centuries-old dance called *Prima* is performed and an offering of the branches of *anfiladas* is made to the Virgen Santísima de la Regalina.

«El Naseiro».

Vivero, Lugo province. This excursion to the hermitage of Nuestra Señora de la Peña de Francia, where a solemn procession is later held, is of both folkloric and gastronomic interest.

«Encierro» or Bull Run.

Cuéllar, Segovia province. Last Sunday in August and the following Monday and Tuesday. The fiesta begins when the fighting bulls that will be fought in the bull ring later in the day are led through the streets. The «run» is over a kilometer long and ends in the ring where the bulls are put into pens. Throughout the fiestas, town clubs and refreshment stands, with constant dancing and singing, are open to everyone.

Fiesta of San Félix Mártir.

Vilafranca del Panadés, Barcelona province. A guild fiesta dating back to the Middle Ages, in 1814 it became a festivity celebrated by the entire population. Splendid popular dances of medieval origin and human-castle building contests. In the evening a procession is held that ends in the Basilica of Santa María.

Montilla-Moriles Wine Harvest.

Montilla, Córdoba province. This gay fiesta includes, among other festivities, the procession of the Virgen de las Viñas («Virgin of the Vineyards»), the blessing of the first must of the year, a contest of wine-making skills, the election of the stewards of honor of the Casa del Inca wine cellar, a carriage parade, and public wine proclamation.

Retaule de San Ermengol.

Seo de Urgel, Lérida province. This is a medieval mystery play—with eight scenes evoking the life, death and miracles of San Ermengol—performed in the cloisters of the city's cathedral since very remote times.

Fiesta of Nuestra Señora la Antigua de Manjavacas.

Mota del Cuervo, Cuenca province. At the beginning of the fiestas, the image of the Virgin is covered and then carried on a platform from the hermitage. When the image arrives at the parish church, it is uncovered and the procession begins. At the end of the fiestas, the Virgin is carried back to the hermitage in the same way she was brought. A picturesque aspect of this procession is the velocity—32 minutes—with which the bearers of the platform (they change shifts as they go) manage to cover the 6 kilometers of the procession.

September Fiestas in Honor of María Santísima de la Sierra.

Cabra, Córdoba province. The Virgen María Santísima de la Sierra is carried by a retinue of riders, attired in Andalusian dress, from her hermitage in Picacho in the sierra to the city. On the following days a parade of carriages with a flower battle is held, as well as sports, bullfighting and folkloric spectacles, ending with the procession of the Patron Saint. Festivals of Spain.

Fiestas of Moors and Christians in Honor of Nuestra Señora de las Virtudes.

Villena, Alicante province. Dating from the 15th century. Festivities begin with the entrance celebration: two thousand participants, divided into 14 groups, wait on the outskirts of the town to receive the Patron Saint when she is brought from her Sanctuary. The battles last two days and end on the Patron Saint's Day, with the triumph of the Christians, after which a solemn procession is held. On the last day of the fiestas at seven in the morning, the farewell celebration is held after which the Virgin is returned to her Sanctuary.

Jerez Wine Harvest Fiesta.

Jerez de la Frontera, Cádiz province. Held since 1948. Each year it is dedicated to a country that consumes wine from Jerez. Aside from the blessing of the wine and must before the image of San Ginés de la Jara—Patron Saint of the region's grape-growers—a sumptuous cavalcade is held, as well as a flamenco festival, wine-making, literary and livestock competitions, livestock exhibits and bullfights.

Moors and Christians.

Caudete, Albacete province. The fiestas of the Virgen de Gracia, are renowned for their typical parades and the enactment in the main square of the town of the traditional *Episodios Caudetanos,* based on a manuscript dating from 588. Flower offering. Blunderbuss procession. Flag display. Participants dressed as Moors and Christians give a gay and picturesque note to the fiesta.

Fiestas of the Madre de Deu de la Salut.

Algemesí, Valencia province. The *maixeranga* (quadrille of men who form a human tower), the *Bastonets* (dancers that beat poles) and *Pastorets* (shepherds) accompany the procession of the Virgin performing traditional Valencian dances to the rhythm of the *colcaina* (a type of flute) and the *tabalet* (timbrel). A major attraction are the human towers formed by the *Muxerangueros.*

Excursion of Nuestra Señora de los Angeles.

Alájar, Huelva province. Celebrated since 1924. A multitude of riders, attired in typical Andalusian dress and accompanied by a band of music and timbrel and flageolet players, go to the Peña de Arias Montano where they pray at the hermitage of Nuestra Señora de los Angeles. On the last day the image of this Virgin is carried in procession in the surrounding countryside.

Fairs and Fiestas of Albacete.

Albacete. They date from 1710, and the Fair was declared of National Commercial Interest in 1933. Festivities begin with a Salve Regina in the Cathedral in honor of the Virgin de los Llanos whose image is then taken to the fair building in a lavish cavalcade. Aside from the celebration of the Festivals of Spain, the fiestas also include popular concerts, sports demonstrations, bullfights, an international art show and an inter-regional exhibit of crafts and artisanship.

Fiestas of Nuestra Señora del Pino.

Villa de Teror, Las Palmas province. Medieval origin. The image of the Virgin is lowered from her place behind the altar in a simulacrum of the descent from heaven, and two days later is raised to her place using the same ingenious procedure.

«Fiesta Mayor» and «Corre de Bou».

Cardona, Barcelona province. The *Corre de Bou,* the fiesta's main attraction, is a bullfighting spectacle dating back to the 15th century: in a square-shaped enclosure set up in front of the Town Hall, hundreds of young men confront the young bulls unarmed and, in case of danger, fling themselves to safety by grabbing one of the ropes hanging over the square. Especially spectacular is the *cargoleta* in which a man inside a straw basket, from which only his head and feet can protrude, waits in the center of the square for the bull to charge.

Excursion of Nuestra Señora de Chilla.

Candeleda, Avila province. Celebrated since the year 1300. The image of the Virgin is taken to the place where she appeared and a mass and sermon are held there. During the following two days *encierros,* or bull runs, are held in which not only young men but also young women run with the bulls that will be fought later in the day.

Patron Saint Fiestas of Santo Cristo and San Vicente Ferrer.

Graus, Huesca province. Of great folkloric interest, they include typical dances with warlike personages such as Caballet and Futaperas; songs called *albada* which are sung at dawn; bullfights and other festivities.

Excursion of the Santísimo Cristo del Caloco.

El Espinar, Segovia province. The fiesta dates back to the 16th century. The image of the Santísimo Cristo del Caloco is returned to its hermitage in procession after the novenary is held in El Espinar. In the atrium of the hermitage typical regional dances known as the *rueda* and the *respingona espinariega* are performed.

Rice Fiesta.

Sueca, Valencia province. Festivities begin with the proclamation of the Rice Queen. Noteworthy is the offering of new spikes to Nuestra Señora de Sales whose Sanctuary is visited by a colorful cavalcade. Prior to this a national *paella* (Valencia's typical rice dish) contest is held which attracts many people from the region.

«America Day» in Asturias.

Oviedo. Dates from 1950. In the morning a mass is held at the University in honor of the Marianist dedication to Spanish solidarity with Spanish America and in homage to mothers of Asturian emigrants. In the afternoon a colorful cavalcade with carriages, bands of music and folkloric groups is held with the participation of groups from numerous countries of South America, some European countries and different areas of the region.

Fiestas of the Wine Harvest of Rioja.

Logroño. They began in 1955. Aside from the high point of the festivity—the blessing of the first must—, a flower battle, a literary contest, a song festival and nighttime entertainment are also held. At the same time the traditional fiestas of San Mateo are celebrated with bullfighting and sports events.

Royal Fair and Fiesta of the Wine Harvest of Condado.

Palma del Condado, Huelva province. The blessing of the year's first must is the major event. Festivities also include floral displays, carriage parades, and flamenco song and dance in the fair stands gaily decorated for the occasion. An important livestock fair is also held.

Fiestas of Nuestra Señora de la Merced.

Barcelona. Created in 1871 in honor of the Virgin de la Merced, declared Patron Saint of the city and diocesis of Barcelona by Pope Pius IX on May 2, 1868. They include religious celebrations, sports and folkloric events, art exhibits as well as literary, music, theater and film festivals.

Excursion in Honor of the Saints and Martyrs Cosme and Damián.

Mieres, Oviedo province. Dating back to time immemorial. The Sanctuary of the Saints where, according to legend, centuries ago a small chest was found with the mortal remains of these saints, is located in the parish of Valdecuna, within the municipal district of Mieres, surrounded by a lovely country setting. After high mass, held at noon, a procession takes place in which hundreds of people pray for their illnesses to disappear or give thanks for the disappearance of sickness. Then, on a much livelier note, regional music breaks out, the dancing begins and visitors are invited to taste the first of the cider harvested in Asturias.

Day of Campóo.

Reinosa, Santander province. Last Sunday in September. The fiesta's origin goes back to 1895. From the early hours of the morning the reveilles played by the band of music and the flageolets, accompanied by giant pasteboard figures can be heard. Contests, carriage parades, folkloric events, round dances. Contestants all wear the typical mountain or country-style costumes of the region.

Patron Saint Fiestas of the Virgin of Vallivana.

Morella, Castellón province. Among the religious acts, especially noteworthy is the Excursion of the Virgin of Vallivana in which the image is carried in a solemn procession from her Sanctuary to Morella. Every six years solemn fiestas, called *Sexenales,* are held. The next ones will take place in 1982.

Wine Harvest Fiestas.

Valdepeñas, Ciudad Real province. Wine tasters' contest. Local contest of *sangría* and lemonade drinks. Cultural and artistic exhibits. Poetry contest. Popular festivities.

AUTUMN

Pilar Fiestas.

Saragossa. First celebrated in the 19th century. The fiestas begin with the Cavalcade of the Proclamation. At the Palacio de la Lonja, the Queen of the Fiestas and her maids of honor are proclaimed. Major events are the offering of flowers to the Virgin in the Basílica del Pilar—by women wearing typical regional costumes—and the procession of the Virgin and Patron Saint of Spain. Festivities also include folkloric parades with carriages and the Official Aragonese Jota Contest.

Shellfish Fest.

El Grove, Pontevedra province. Second Sunday in October. A typical regional excursion is held with Galician dances and choruses, during which a live shellfish contest is held as well as contests for the best seasoning of dishes prepared with shellfish.

«As San Lucas».

Mondoñedo, Lugo province. These are the most important livestock (horses, mules and donkeys) fairs held in northwestern Spain. A wide variety of crafts articles are also sold. The fiestas have conserved many of their original medieval features.

Excursion of the Virgen de Valme.

Dos Hermanas, Seville province. Dates from 1894. Celebrated in honor of the Virgin whose image is carried in a gaily adorned wagon from Dos Hermanas to the hermitage. During the procession—some eight kilometers—riders dressed in Andalusian style form a retinue to accompany the Virgin. During the rest stops on the journey singing and dancing break out. Mass is held at the Cortijo de Cuarte and then the Virgin is returned to her original point of departure.

Saffron Fiestas.

Consuegra, Toledo province. Celebrated since 1963 during the saffron harvest; especially interesting is the pruning of the flowers, after which a regional folklore show is held.

«La Encamisá».

Torrejoncillo, Cáceres province. A multitude of riders covered with sheets head from their houses to that of the major-domo where they receive the lantern they will carry during the *Encamisá.* Then they take off at a gallop to the main square. This fiesta is held to commemorate the battle the town won thanks to a snowfall.

Midnight Mass.

Labastida, Alava province. Dates from the Middle Ages. Minutes before midnight, twelve shepherds and their leader meet in front of the Town Hall accompanied by the grandfather and the shepherdess, each carrying a sheep and the Christ Child respectively. The shepherds stand before the mayor and the councilmen singing songs and then, still singing, accompany them to the church where, after greeting the priest, they perform a dance beating their rods on the ground; songs and dances alternate as mass is celebrated. After mass the shepherds light a bonfire near the church and pretend to prepare a broth which they give to the Christ Child carried by the shepherdess.